PRACTICAL Sailing

Wendy Fitzpatrick

Ward Lock Limited·London

Acknowledgments

I would like to thank Malcolm McKeag for writing Chapter 4, Ingrid Holford for her contribution to Chapter 10, and Mike Fitzpatrick for the ocean racing section of Chapter 12. I would also like to thank Peter Cook of *Yachts and Yachting* for the use of additional material and the staff of *Yachts and Yachting* for the use of their photographic library.

© Ward Lock Limited 1979

First published in Great Britain in 1979 by Ward Lock Limited, 116 Baker Street, London W1M 2BB, a member of the Pentos Group.

Designed by Mel Saunders

House editor Gill Upton

Text filmset in Baskerville by Rembrandt Filmsetting Ltd.

Printed and bound in Hong Kong by South China Printing Co. Ltd

British Library Cataloguing in Publication Data

Practical Sailing
  1. Sailing
  I. Fitzpatrick, Wendy
  797.1´24   GV811

ISBN 0-7063-5765-5

Contents

Introduction

Sailing is thought to be amongst the most popular participant sports in the world. So few countries have really rigid registration of boats that it is impossible to make accurate analyses of the number in commission – even less, the number of people who sail them.

But then, it has to be a participant sport: its spectator appeal is strictly limited and outside Australia, New Zealand and a few sailing-orientated local newspapers, press coverage of even prestige events is minimal. Those who enjoy watching a sailing race can only be those who understand the niceties of the manoeuvres involved. And those who understand what they are watching would far rather be out there sailing themselves. Mass-start classic races attract their share of spectators and well-wishers – all, notice, in their own or a friend's waterborne transport.

It is the pursuit of the individualist, the man who hates to be pigeon-holed, and to him we offer apologies for attempting to do just that in the following pages. For any explanation of the sport must identify its different branches. One may as well try to describe athletics without mentioning the different track and field events and the types of athlete who excel in each.

1 Types of boat

Sailing – basking on the sun-drenched deck of a graceful schooner, sipping a rum punch? Possibly. Squelching exhausted up a muddy slipway in the rain, pulling a waterlogged dinghy? More probable.

Sailing – or yachting, or boating, or watersport – is not a single sport. It may not even be a sport at all, for there are many thousands of addicts who spend all their leisure time afloat without ever answering the call of the starter's gun. There are others again who derive greatest enjoyment from their boat by staying ashore and working on her, rather than actually sailing her. Oh yes, *her*. Some owners of impersonal glassfibre one-designs may well refer to their boats as *it* but to those who lavish love and attention, *she* is undeniably feminine.

The casual cruising man, whether his craft be 10ft or 100ft (3m or 30m) long, and the near-professional ocean racing addict may not appear to be the same breed of animal, but they are united by a common addiction: the challenge of wind and wave. United, too, in their choice of *après*-sail enjoyment. They may foregather in a waterside bar, in a tin-shack sailing club, in the comfort or discomfort of another cruiser's cabin or in a palatial yacht club but their singular aim is to hold a post mortem on the day's sailing over a cooling draught (or two).

It is the depth of his pocket which dictates a sailor's level of involvement, but his own personality which governs the type of sailing he chooses.

He may start his sailing career as a crew member for an experienced boat owner – a sensible approach, this, learning at someone else's expense – or he may buy his own boat from the outset and learn by his own ghastly mistakes. If he takes the latter course he will very probably choose a dinghy in the first instance; as it happens, a wise choice, for learning to sail in a responsive small boat is the very best grounding a skipper can have, whatever he may progress to in subsequent years.

Sailing *can* involve sipping a planter's punch aboard a luxury schooner in the Caribbean. It's more likely to involve this.

'. . . learn by his own ghastly mistakes.' *William G. Rowntree*

The elegant Dragon is perhaps the epitome of the racing keelboat.
Bermuda News Bureau

The 20ft (6m) Tornado is the Olympic catamaran. *Yachts & Yachting*

Day Sailers

Taken literally, the term 'day sailer' could cover all boats which are not actually used for overnight passage-making – in fact, the majority of pleasure craft. It is generally understood, however, to refer to the type of boat which has no accommodation: the dinghy, the smaller multihulls, the open keelboats and the off-the-beach boats such as the so-called sailing surfboards.

Dinghies: A dinghy is a small, open boat. It can be a 7ft-8ft (2-2.5m) yacht tender which boasts no more than a central seat (thwart) and a pair of oars but we are concerned here with sailing boats. A sailing dinghy needs three things which a rowing dinghy does not possess: sails to provide the motive power; a rudder for steering; and a centreboard which can be lowered below the boat to help her to slice through the water without being blown sideways.

Keelboats: Keelboats tend to start where dinghies stop – the upper size range of the dinghy scale, about 18ft-20ft (5.5m-6m), is coincidentally the lower end of the keelboat range. Whereas the dinghy relies on the weight of the crew to keep her upright, the keelboat's stability is provided by a fixed and ballasted keel which, unlike the dinghy's centreboard, cannot be housed within the hull of the boat. Consequently keelboats tend to be kept on moorings.

Multihulls: *Catamarans* are probably the best known type of multihull, with their twin hulls joined by beams fore and aft. These hulls may be identical or asymmetric, that is, a mirror-image of each other, and the space between will be filled by a solid or fabric bridgedeck or trampoline.

A proa also has two hulls, but one is very much smaller than the other – in effect merely an outrigger to provide stability to the single, main hull. This outrigger may be used to leeward, as a float, or to windward where the crew will provide the necessary ballast for balance. Whichever method is adopted, it remains constant, so a ballasted windward outrigger will never be used as a leeward float. Thus, it is not possible to change direction in the same way as in a conventional boat: the whole rig of a proa must be reversed and a rudder is needed at each end of the main hull to enable it to sail either backwards or forwards, depending on the direction of the wind.

A trimaran has three hulls. The two outriggers are relatively small and it is usually only the leeward one which is in contact with the water, acting as a float, while the windward one is just kissing the surface, awaiting its turn to become the leeward float when the boat changes course.

The Drascombe Lugger is a good, sturdy, characterful day sailing boat. *Martin Treadway*

The Windsurfer – little more than a surfboard with a sail on top – has enjoyed a meteoric rise to fame. *Bahamas News Bureau*

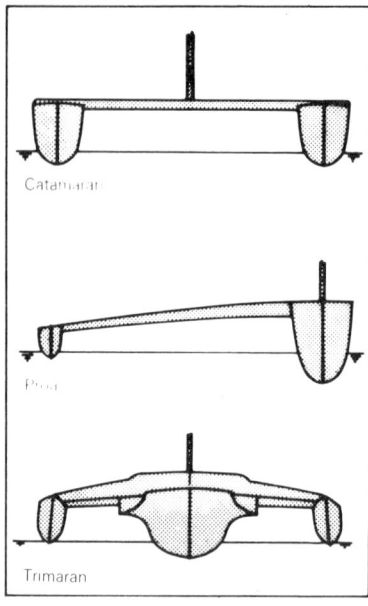

1.1 Multi-hull cross-sections. (*top*) A racing or day-sailing catamaran. The mast is stepped on the centreline on one of the beams that join the two hulls. (*centre*) A proa has one main hull and a single outrigger which is usually to leeward when the boat is sailing. To change tacks the rig is reversed and the boat steered from the other end. (*bottom*) A cruising trimaran has accommodation in the main hull and stowage in the outriggers. In large trimarans the outriggers may also be used for accommodation.

Off-the-Beach Boats: board boats, sailing planks, sailing surfboards, are just some of the often derogatory names given to a generation of pure fun boats designed for simplicity of rig and ease of handling and preparation for the water. Their very simplicity has led in many cases to the adoption of strict rules with the result that several classes enjoy extensive racing calendars world-wide; the more adventurous (or more heavily subsidized!) now organize regattas to which it is not necessary to transport a boat, all boats being provided by the local agent or host club because all can be guaranteed to be identical, from the Bahamas to Bangkok.

The Family Cruiser

Early cruising boats were built along the lines of traditional fishing and working boats. Some still are, for these designs have proved themselves over many, many years to be seaworthy, handy and robust. But a new generation of sailors accustomed to labour-saving luxury in the home has demanded at least a degree of home comfort in the waterborne weekend retreat and in consequence a new generation of roomy little glassfibre cruising boats has grown up to meet the depth (or shallowness) of father's pocket and the size of his family.

Some cruisers as small as 20ft (6m) will profess to have sleeping accommodation for four or even five. But something has to be sacrificed for this voluminous accommodation and that something is often sailing ability so that many 'cruisers' are little more than rather slow day-sailers with accommodation – and usually only sleeping accommodation at that, for stowage of a full crew's gear in this type of boat is often a problem.

But there are many excellent modern cruising boats looking like, and sailing nearly as well as, their racing sisters; for the rating rules of the 1970s offshore racer favour big, light, beamy boats with plenty of scope for generous accommodation below.

The Offshore Racer

The very first ocean races were between the giants – the 100ft and 200ft (about 30m and 60m) schooners which the wealthy aristocracy of the era built as private yachts, along the lines of the commercial fast trading ships of the day. It was a case of first past the post wins: handicaps were unknown. During the 1800s and early this century rating rules – rules of measurement – were developed in the leading yacht racing countries. In Britain they tended to favour long, narrow designs (so narrow at one stage that they came to be known as 'plank on edge') while in America wider, lightweight boats developed, often with centreboards.

Now there is an International Offshore Rule which is constantly updated and which has led to the development of a dinghy-like hull, light in weight with generous beam and plenty of freeboard. The modern racing rig features enormous genoas, tiny mainsails and a multitude of downwind sails to complement the spinnaker, glorying in such names as big-boy and blooper. Under the water the long keel has given way to truncated fin keels with separate rudders.

The racing boat's generous space below deck, however, is not devoted to luxurious living. The crew will have the lightest possible terylene pipecots (a cross between a bunk and a hammock), the very minimum of galley and toilet facilities (no pumping out: holes in a racing hull are taboo, for their associated fittings create drag) but acres of space will be devoted to the stowage

In among the offshore fleet. *Ajax News Photos*

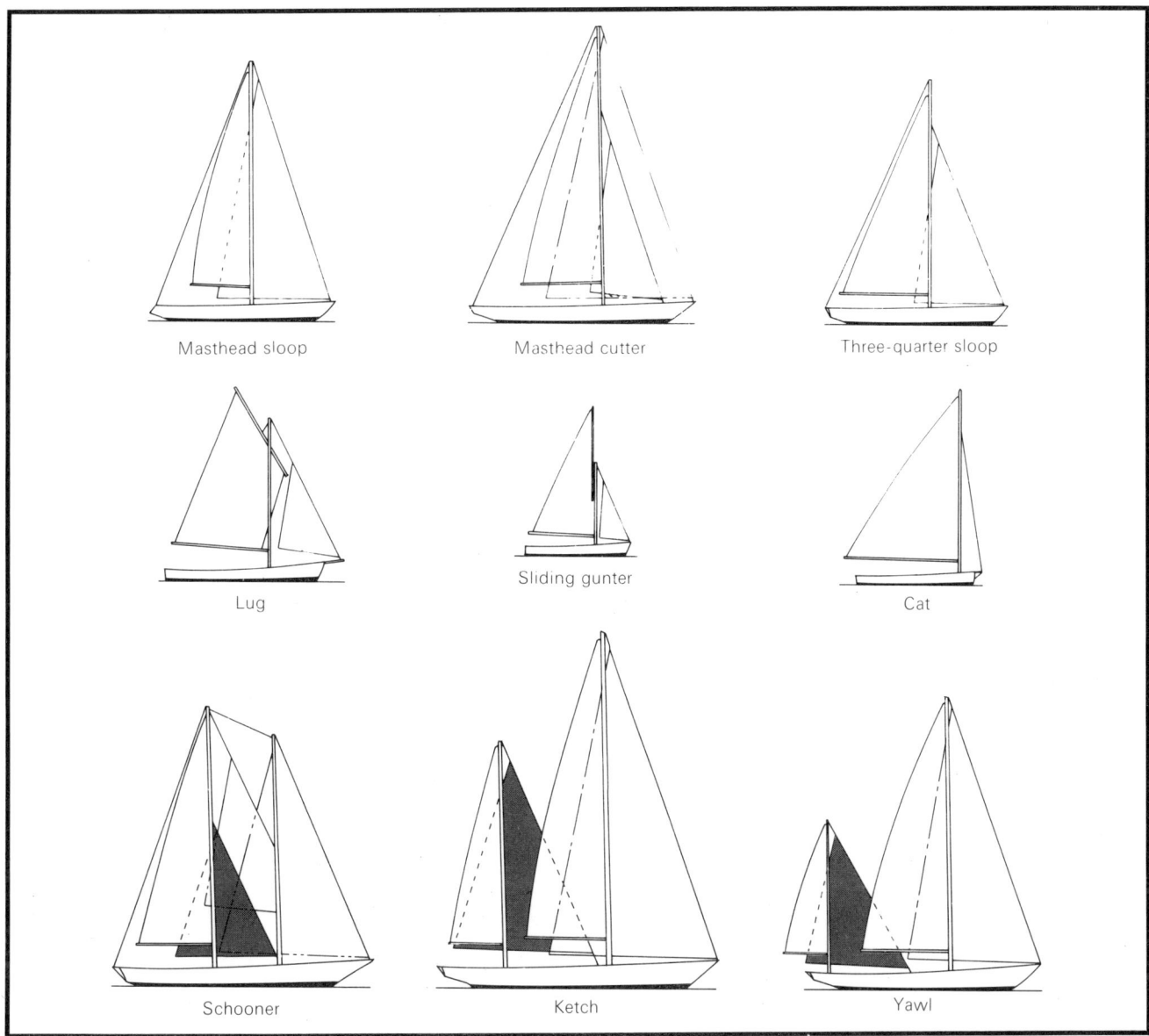

Masthead sloop

Masthead cutter

Three-quarter sloop

Lug

Sliding gunter

Cat

Schooner

Ketch

Yawl

1.2 Rigs.

of sails. The navigator, alone, has a degree of luxury. His chart table is well equipped and sited in the most comfortable, driest part of the boat, reflecting the importance of his role.

Old Timers

There's no denying the romance of the oldies, whether they be graceful racing yachts, schooners from a bygone age, workboats or chunky gaff cruisers. They are history in action, a sense that after all perhaps all is not yet lost to the Great God Plastic.

But their practical appeal is limited. They may be heavily constructed hence slow, they demand constant attention to maintain them in good condition and their traditional gear is often too rugged for soft, city-slicker hands. Fortunately there is a minority of boat owners who can afford the time and money to devote to their upkeep – fortunately, too, there are others who build along traditional lines so that they may enjoy the romance of the old and the convenience of the new.

Rigs

Rigs differ as much as the boats they drive. For all practical purposes, the square-rigger has disappeared, recurring only occasionally in the guise of sail training ships of countries whose budget allows them to commission large vessels for their young cadets' training. Demanding of much manpower, the square rigged ship is an ideal sail-trainer.

But if the square rigged ship is with us no more, the

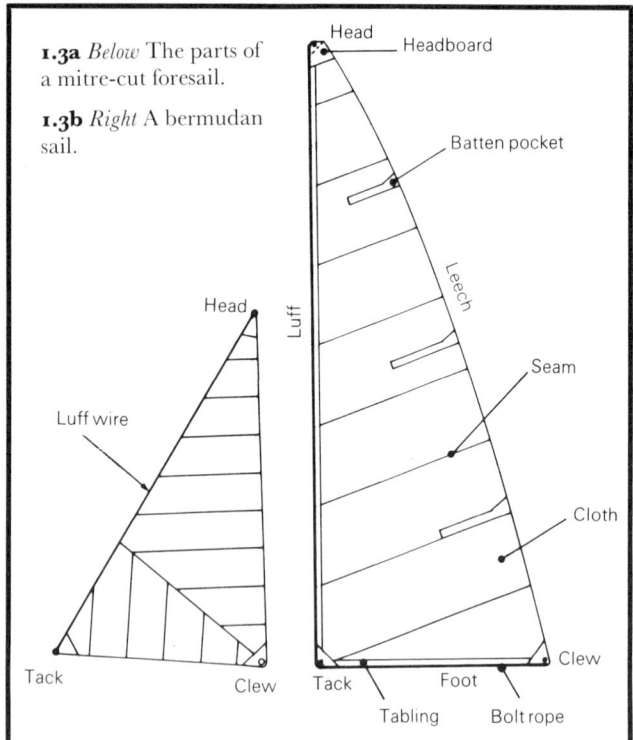

1.3a *Below* The parts of a mitre-cut foresail.

1.3b *Right* A bermudan sail.

Some folk cruise from marina berth to marina berth. Others like to get away from it all and enjoy the tranquillity of a deserted backwater, with only the seabirds for company. *Martin Treadway*

squaresail is still to be seen – perhaps as part of the sail wardrobe of a large schooner or even on a boat whose long-distance cruising ground is in the trade winds.

The most common rig afloat today is the **bermudan sloop** – bermudan referring to a triangular, as opposed to a quadrilateral or gaff-rigged mainsail; sloop indicating the presence of a single mainsail and a single foresail. A sloop may be said to be masthead-rigged, three-quarter rigged or one of many other variants, the dimension referring to the height of the top of the foresail in relation to the top of the mast.

Add a second, smaller foresail inside the first and you have a **cutter.**

Add a second, smaller, mast aft of the mainmast and you have a ketch or a yawl: a **ketch** if the second – mizzen – mast is stepped forward of the rudder post; a **yawl** if the mizzen mast is stepped abaft the rudder post: a fine distinction and one which is difficult to draw at a distance. There is further definition governed by the purpose of the mizzen: that a yawl uses the sail more as an aid to the rudder, for steering the yacht, whereas a ketch relies on its driving force to complement her rig.

If the second mast is the mainmast the boat is **schooner** rigged. Ketches, yawls and schooners may each set a staysail between the two masts – hoisted to the main or mizzen mast and tacked down on to the deck aft of the fore or mainmast.

A **gaff** mainsail is a quadrilateral sail whose top is laced to a gaff spar. Whereas most modern sails are made from modern synthetic cloth such as Terylene or

The British training ship TS 'Royalist' at anchor in Poole Harbour. The ladder-like constructions are ratlines and enable the crew members to climb aloft to handle the immense amount of rigging which is necessary on even a small square-rigger. *Frank Briley*

Dacron, the chances are that gaff sails, even brand new ones, are still made of canvas or flax. The luff of the gaff mainsail slides up and down the mast on hoops – as may the sliding **gunter** rig whose gaff stands nearly vertical to produce, in effect, a triangular sail.

A **lug** sail is a quadrilateral sail whose gaff – and sometimes the boom as well – sets partly forward of the mast. A standing lug, as its name implies, remains hoisted while the boat is manoeuvring but a dipping lug is lowered when the boat tacks, to be rehoisted and reset on the other side of the mast.

2 Why the boat moves

It is not difficult to accept that a boat can sail with the wind blowing from directly astern, simply pushing her forward. But she can sail at other angles to the wind, as close as 35° in some cases. How?

Consider for a moment the case of a boat with a single sail, the sort of rig which will be found on many singlehanded dinghies. The easiest way to explain how this triangle of cloth produces sufficient drive to push a boat through the resisting water is to draw a parallel with the way in which an aeroplane is lifted by its wings – the two phenomena are, after all, about as likely as each other.

The wing of a 'plane has more curvature on its upper surface than its lower surface. As it moves forward, air streams across both surfaces, the air which takes the upper route having to travel faster over the longer distance in order to meet up at the trailing edge with its travelling companion which opted for the lower route. This speed difference causes a drop in pressure on the upper surface of the wing and this results in lift. As the aeroplane's speed increases, the air travels faster over the wing and lift increases until it is sufficient to raise the whole weight of the plane off the ground.

A similar thing happens over the surface of a boat's sail. It assumes an aerofoil shape as it fills with wind, the air travelling round the leeward side must travel faster than the air travelling round the windward side, pressure drops to leeward and lift is created.

It is the channelling of this lift to create forward drive which dictates the shape of a boat's hull. The wind's energy is trying to push the boat sideways; it is the boat designer's job to make sure that she moves forward.

Next time you have a bath, place the wet soap on the wet tile surround and press down on it. It shoots forward, because it is prevented from moving in the direction in which you were pressing by the presence of the bath.

Now hold a knife blade in a bowl of water and move it first with the narrow edge leading, then with the flat side leading. The flat side of the knife resists lateral movement, in the same way that the keel or centreboard of a boat resists lateral movement – or leeway.

Variations in the rig and the way in which it is controlled are the most important considerations affecting performance, for the rig is the engine of a sailing boat.

For any given wind strength the greatest possible driving force must be extracted from the rig. To achieve

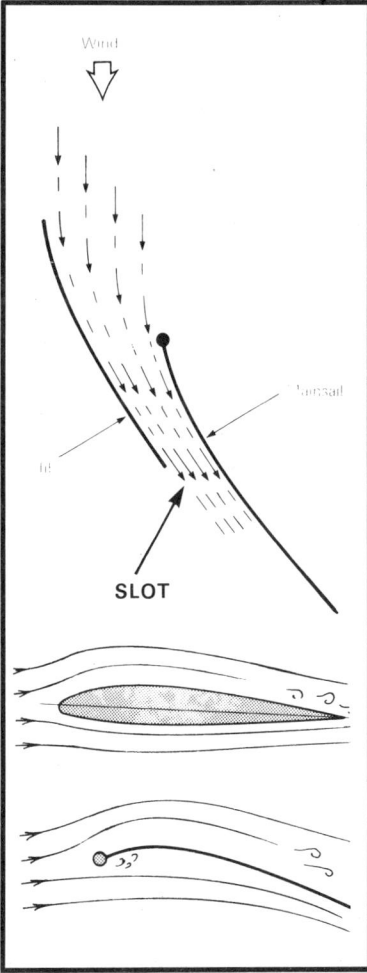

2.1a Slot effect. The jib concentrates the airflow over the leeward side of the mainsail and causes it to accelerate. This produces a drop in pressure which results in an increase in drive.

2.1b (*centre*) Cross-section of an aeroplane wing. The air moves faster over the upper surface producing a drop in pressure that results in lift. (*bottom*) Similarly, wind travels faster over the leeward side of a sail than it does over the windward side producing a drop in pressure to leeward that results in forward drive.

. . . not difficult to appreciate that a boat can literally be 'pushed' along downwind. *Studio 77*

The big, overlapping genoa is driving this Flying Dutchman to windward. It is backwinding the mainsail at its forward part and the mast is bending in the gusts to open the leech of the mainsail and spill excess wind. *National Foto Persbureau*

each other and work harmoniously together, and second with the crew, who must adjust and control the rig to suit the prevailing conditions.

Just as different shapes of aeroplane wing are called for to cater for different speeds and weights of aircraft, so the shape and cut of a boat's sails must suit her speed and weight, the sea conditions in which she will be sailed, and the weight of the crew. We have seen how drive is produced from a single sail by the air moving faster over the leeward side than the windward side, which results in a drop in pressure to leeward. Add another sail, the jib, ahead of the mainsail and when both sails are sheeted correctly, the airflow over the leeward side of the mainsail is directed with greater velocity and travels further before it breaks away in turbulence. This phenomenon is known as slot effect and one of the most important factors of sail performance is achieving the correct slot for the rig.

We should digress here to point out the fallacy of the apparently logical example which opened this chapter. When the wind is aft and the spinnaker is set, it is not sufficient for the keen crew to lay back and relax and allow themselves to be 'pushed' along downwind. There will be a pocket of dead air in the spinnaker which will enhance neither its drive nor its ability to set well. Instead, the boat's performance will be improved immensely if the spinnaker is sheeted so that the airflow is across the sail, in the manner of the fore-and-aft sails.

Even on smooth water the wind varies constantly in strength and direction and the rig has to adjust to this continuously if a smooth airflow is to be maintained. Changes in direction are catered for by the crew trimming the sheets; variations in strength by weight adjustment and sail trim. As the wind increases the crew move further to windward (or the boat's ballast keel helps to resist the heeling force) until they are applying the maximum righting moment possible by sitting out or trapezing in order to keep the boat level. When the heeling effect of the wind becomes greater than the righting moment that can be applied, some wind must be spilled from the sails.

The usual way of doing this in an isolated gust of wind is for the helmsman to ease the mainsheet, but if the increase in the strength of the wind is permanent the sail area will need to be reduced, either by reefing or by changing to a smaller sail. In smaller racing boats a degree of automatic adjustment is built in to the mast and sail combination: the top of the mast is allowed to flex a controlled amount as a gust hits, bending off to leeward and opening the leech of the mainsail (also the slot) to spill the wind which is momentarily in excess of the crew's requirements.

Efficiency in the rig, while vital, is not everything. Marry it to the right hull shape and you will have a fast

this a smooth flow of air must be maintained which at all times produces the optimum forward drive. The responsibility for achieving this rests first with the sparmaker and sailmaker, whose products must match

With all the devotion of a housewife tending the family wash, the crew of a big racing keelboat pack away the sail wardrobe. Tidiness on board is of paramount importance to cope with the enormous number of sails which are carried. *Silvio Mursia*

The curved gaff spar, tucked-up bow and leeboards are part of the charm of the traditional Dutch sailing boat. *John Watney*

An Olympic three-man Soling keelboat going great guns on a shy reach under maxi-spinnaker
Wendy Fitzpatrick

An interesting mix of squaresails and fore and aft sails on the Irish 'Phoenix'. *John Watney*

boat; marry it to a heavy or shapeless hull and the result will be a boat which will not, as the saying goes, sail out of its own way.

The right hull shape, this being an individualist's sport, is right only for its intended purpose. There is a tremendous variety of 'right' hull shapes in the sailing world and still one comes across those which are glaringly 'wrong'. But whatever its purpose, a hull must conform to certain design parameters if it is to become a worthwhile boat.

It must be fair – that is, free from bumps, hollows and sudden distortions which are abhorrent both to the eye of the beholder and to the water which must flow round them. It must have fine forward sections to enable it to nose through the sea: as a general rule, but by no means free from exception, the finer a boat the faster and wetter she will be. It must have sufficient buoyancy to support the weight of the boat, her equipment and her crew without sinking below her designed waterline.

Archimedes taught us that the weight of any object floating in water equals the weight of the water that it displaces. Hence, a light-displacement boat which weighs less than a heavy-displacement hull displaces less water and in theory needs less sail to drive her at the same speed.

The centre of gravity of an object is the point where the components of its weight may be assumed to be concentrated. The force of gravity acts downwards through this point. But water exerts pressure perpendicular to the immersed surface of an object and the resultant upward force is called buoyancy.

The centre of buoyancy is the centre of gravity of the volume displaced by and having the same shape as the immersed part of the boat.

When a boat floats freely in calm water with no external force applied, the weight of the boat acting vertically downwards through its centre of gravity is opposed by buoyancy acting vertically upwards along the same line through the centre of buoyancy.

Weight is equal to displacement which is equal to buoyancy. This is why a boat floats. If the all-up weight is increased, the object sinks lower in the water, the upward pressure of the water on the hull increases and buoyancy also increases. This is what happens when the crew load themselves and their weekend goodies onto a moored boat. If weight exceeds buoyancy, the boat sinks.

Stability

A boat must be stable, that is, she must float level in the water when no external forces are applied. When an external force is applied that causes the boat to heel – for example, the pressure of the wind in the sails – the

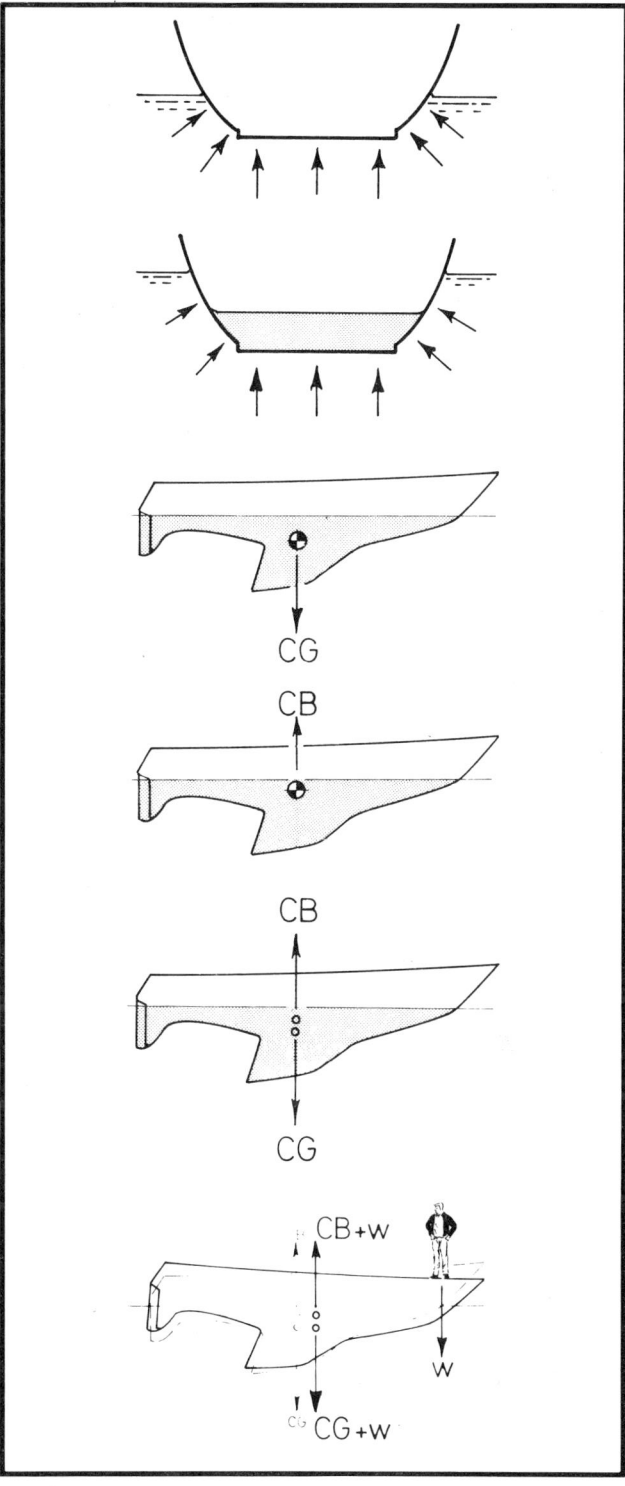

2.2 (*from top*) An empty bowl displaces relatively little water; when water is added, the bowl sinks lower displacing more water, the weight of a boat acts downwards through its centre of gravity; the buoyancy of a boat acts upwards through its centre of buoyancy; when no external forces are applied, the centre of buoyancy and centre of gravity lie on the same vertical line; the combined centre of gravity of man and boat moves foward as he moves. The trim changes to align the centre of buoyancy with the centre of gravity's new position.

2.3 Righting a capsized dinghy; crew members should be clear of the mainsail. Standing on the centreboard and pulling on a line attached to the starboard side brings the dinghy upright, head to wind.

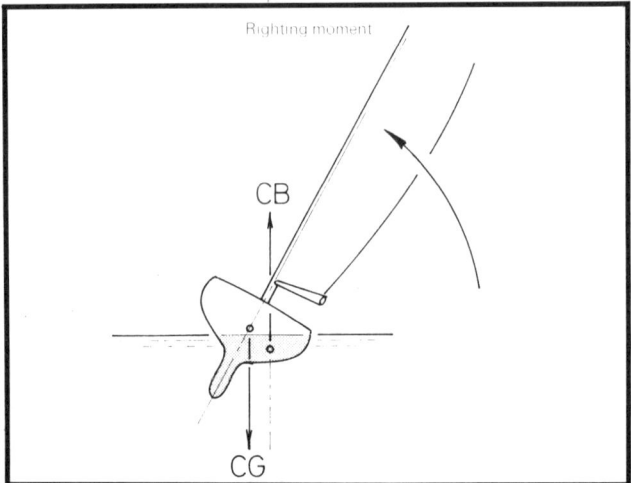

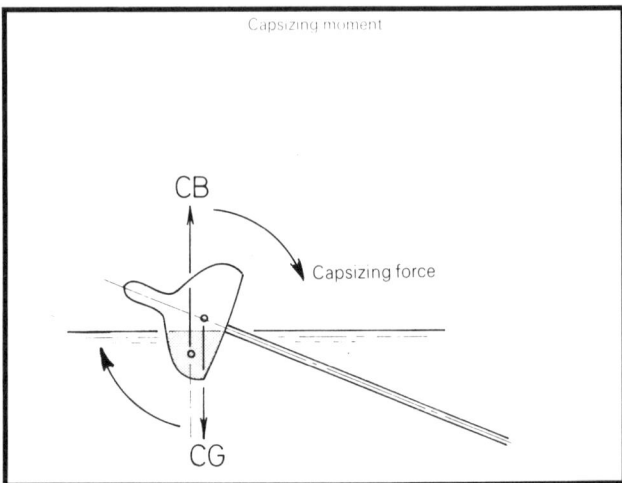

The couple generated by forces acting through the centre of buoyancy and centre of gravity either tends to right the boat (**2.4**) or capsize it (**2.5**).

position of the centre of gravity relative to that of the centre of buoyancy must be such that the weight of the boat acting downwards through the centre of gravity, and the buoyancy acting upwards through the centre of buoyancy, tend to return her to the vertical. This is called the righting moment and the greater the hor-izontal separation of the centres of gravity and buoy-ancy, the greater the righting moment. Occasionally a boat will be knocked over so far that she reaches the point where the downward action of gravity and the upward action of buoyancy tend to make her turn turtle – she is, in other words, subjected to a capsizing moment.

In determining stability the major factor at small angles of heel with most boats is the shift of the centre of buoyancy away from the line of the centre of gravity, thus increasing the length of the righting arm. As a boat heels further, the centre of buoyancy moves less and the major factor becomes the position of the centre of gravity. The lower it is, the further away it will be from the centre of buoyancy and the greater will be the righting couple. So stability depends on the length of the righting arm which is the lateral separation bet-ween the vertical lines passing through the centres of gravity and buoyancy.

In keelboats and cruising yachts the bottom of the keel is usually ballasted with lead or cast iron to achieve a low position for the centre of gravity. An unballasted, flat-bottomed hull will have high initial stability but the stability will reduce as the angle of heel increases, while a narrow, ballasted hull may have a very low initial stability, which will increase until it reaches a maximum when the mast is horizontal.

Extreme examples of stability are, on the one hand, a narrow, deeply veed hull with high ballast ratio and on the other, a completely unballasted catamaran. On the one hand, a low centre of gravity and, subsequently, the maximum righting moment when the mast is horizontal: on the other a very high inherent initial stability which reduces on heeling as the righting arm is shortened and results ultimately in an equally high measure of stability in the inverted position.

Speed

Because a boat is required to move forward through the water, not sideways, the aim of the designer is to reduce forward resistance to a minimum while ensuring that there is sufficient resistance to lateral movement.

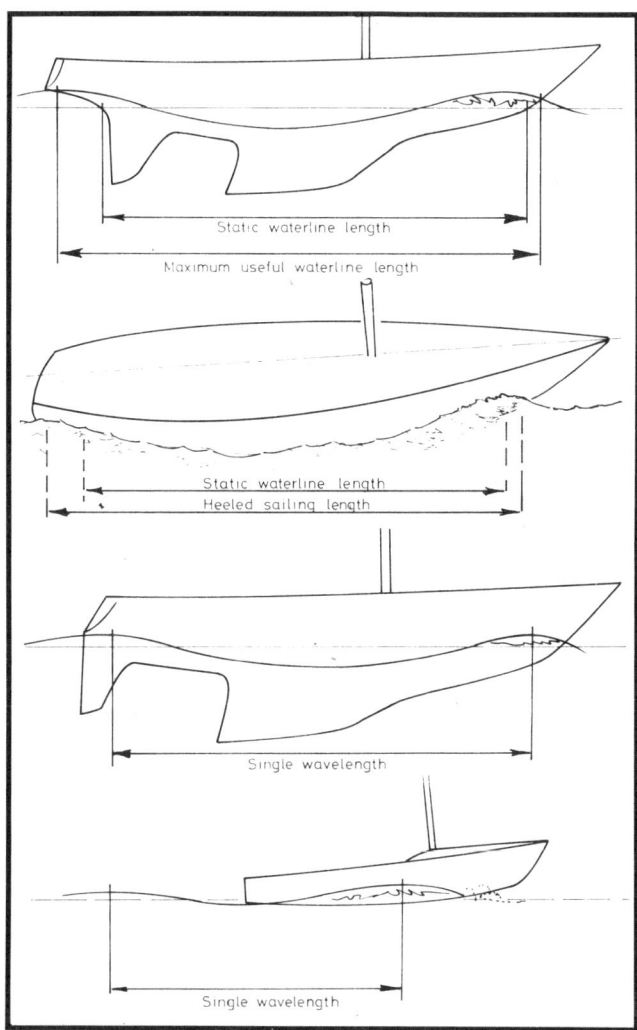

2.6 Effective waterline length. *Bottom* Displacement speeds.

A lightweight dinghy can lift on to its own bow wave and start to plane, travelling much faster than its theoretical displacement speed. This is a Topper. *Martin Treadway*

The principal factors affecting forward movement can be apportioned to wave making, hull drag and skin friction. As a boat moves through the water waves form along its length. As speed increases the waves grow longer until there is one wave crest at the bow and another at the stern with a trough in between. As this point is approached there is a rapid build-up of resistance for little additional increase in speed. The hull cannot make a bigger wave owing to the limits of its length and so tries to climb uphill out of the trough and surmount its own bow wave. Displacement boats are unable to do this and have therefore reached the limit of their performance. Dinghies and fast powerboats, on the other hand, can climb out of their own wave trough but to do so they have to surf over the surface of the water, planing. Once they are planing, resistance to forward motion drops and so speed can increase rapidly. However, displacement boats whose top speed is restricted by their length in smooth water can exceed this speed when sailing in big seas as they surf down the face of a wave.

A good illustration of the wave formation around a displacement keelboat. *William G. Rowntree*

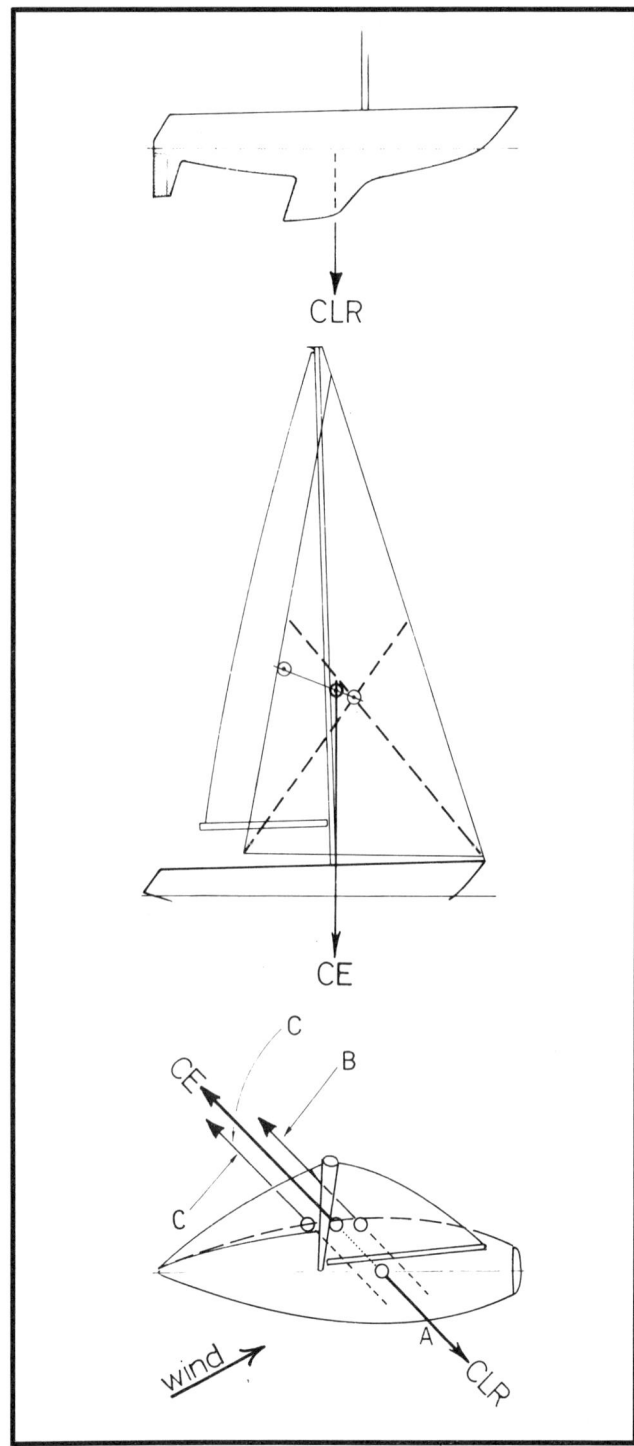

For any hull moving through the water the maximum displacement speed, as opposed to planing speed that it can achieve, in knots, is around 1.4 times the square root of its waterline length, in feet (or in metres multiplied by 3.28, the conversion factor). The maximum theoretical speed of a 16ft (4.8m) dinghy is

$$1.4 \times \sqrt{16} = 1.4 \times 4 = 5.6 \text{ knots}$$
$$(1.4 \times \sqrt{4.8 \times 3.28} = 1.4 \times 3.96 = 5.55 \text{ knots})$$

For a keelboat with a waterline of 36ft (11m) it would be

$$1.4 \times \sqrt{36} = 1.4 \times 6 = 8.4 \text{ knots}$$
$$(1.4 \times \sqrt{11 \times 3.28} = 1.4 \times 6 = 8.4 \text{ knots})$$

So the maximum displacement speed varies as the square root of the waterline length. In the examples, increasing the waterline length from 16ft to 36ft (5m-11m) – more than doubling it – results in only a 50% increase in potential displacement speed.

By giving a boat overhangs fore and aft the effective waterline length is increased, for as the bow and stern waves approach their maximum height, the boat sits lower in the water and the waves move out towards the ends of the boat. Also the waterline length increases as the boat heels. So in calculating the maximum displacement speed of a particular hull it is the effective waterline length, rather than the designed waterline length, that matters.

In a displacement hull – that is, one which is not capable of surmounting its own wave trough and breaking on to the plane – the designer will usually aim for the longest effective waterline length coupled with a hull shape that will reach its maximum speed as easily as possible. A fine-lined racing boat may reach its maximum displacement speed in only 10 knots of wind whereas a chunky cruiser of similar waterline length may need twice that wind strength to reach the same speed. The maximum theoretical speed of both boats is the same: all that varies is the force required to enable each to achieve that speed.

Hull drag is the resistance of the hull to forward movement caused by the shape of the immersed portion of the hull. At one time it was thought that a fast hull had to be very slim and that a beamy hull would inevitably be slow, but this theory has been disproved to a considerable extent in recent years.

Skin friction is the drag produced by the movement of water over the immersed area of the boat and is in proportion to the wetted area. Keeping this wetted area as low as possible can help to reduce resistance.

What do people mean by a 'well balanced' boat?

2.7a (*top*) The centre of lateral resistance is the point about which a boat turns. **2.7b** (*centre*) The CE of a sail is the point through which the wind forces act. To find the CE of a sail plan first find the centres of effort of the individual sails and join these two points with a line. Then divide the line in proportion to the areas of each sail. **2.7c** (*bottom*) The separation of the lines of action through the CE and the CLR decide the balance of the boat. When the lines of action correspond, A, the boat is perfectly balanced. When the line of action through the CE is aft of that through the CLR, B, the boat carries weather helm; when it is forward of that through the CLR, C, the boat carries lee helm.

The hull turns about a point known as the centre of lateral resistance (CLR) which is the effective centre of the area of the underwater profile of the boat. The wind force on a sail can be considered as acting through a point known as the centre of effort (CE) – for a triangular sail the CE lies on a line drawn from one corner to the centre of the opposite side. If lines are drawn from two corners, the point where they cross is the CE. Each sail has its own CE and the combined CE for two sails can be found by drawing a line between the two centres of effort and dividing it in proportion to the individual areas of the two sails.

If the CE is aligned exactly with the CLR, the boat will be perfectly balanced. But if the CE lies aft of the CLR, the pressure of the wind tends to turn the stern away from and the bows towards the wind. To counteract this and in order to steer a straight course, the helmsman has to keep the tiller to windward – he will say that the boat carries weather helm. A small amount of weather helm is acceptable because it imparts a degree of feel to the boat. If it is excessive the helmsman will tire quickly and the rudder, held over at an angle, acts as a brake. If the CE is forward of the CLR, the boat tries to bear away continuously and is said to carry lee helm.

Usually adjustment to balance can be made by moving the position of the CE forward or aft – unless the overall balance between hull and rig is disastrously wrong. Excessive weather helm can be corrected by reducing the area of the mainsail or increasing the area of the headsail, thus moving the CE forward and closer to the CLR. The reverse is true to correct excess lee helm: the area of the mainsail must be increased or that of the headsail reduced to move the CE further aft.

Thus, in strong winds, it is often not sufficient to reef the mainsail. To maintain balance it is usually necessary to set a smaller jib.

Construction

From the earliest canoes which were hollowed out of tree trunks, the traditional boatbuilding material has been wood. Wood can be bent, cut, fastened and fashioned; it is resilient and elastic, available in all grades from hard to soft; used to be abundant and, unlike some modern boatbuilding materials, it floats.

Waterproof glues were unheard of until mid-way through this century, so boats had to rely on the perfect fit of their planking to keep the water out, with only the minimum of help from filler and caulking compounds. Hence traditional building methods rely on the wood swelling – or taking up – after launching to close any gaps. A boat laid up over the winter would always be expected to leak a little until her dried-out planks had

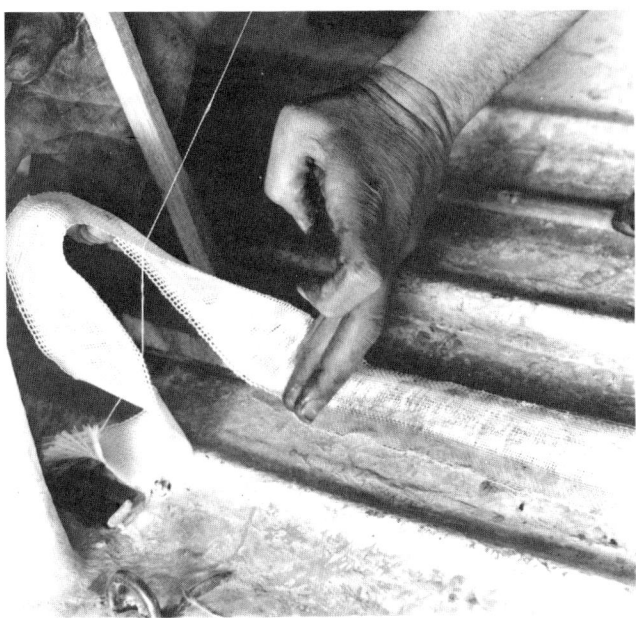
One way to stiffen the flat panels of a glassfibre hull is to run a layer of woven glass tape over foam ribs.

taken up at the beginning of each season. This is one reason why wintering in a mud berth is popular among traditionalists: the hull planks have no chance to shrink through drying out and the soft mud forms a cradle to support the boat.

With the advent of waterproof glue during World War II marine plywood became a viable proposition and with it a whole range of building methods to suit the mass production boatyard and the amateur home builder.

Glassfibre – or, to give it its full name, glass reinforced plastics – which is now so widely accepted, was virtually unknown twenty years ago. It was first hailed by builders of small dinghies, who built the bad as well as the good in those early days. The material's need to be stiffened to prevent flexing on large flat areas was overlooked by a few builders. Others simply used a lot of glassfibre to achieve the necessary stiffness and some heavy boats resulted. But soon all manner of lightweight core stiffening was incorporated, such as end-grain balsa wood, foam, carbon fibre and even tubes of paper or glassfibre itself.

Other plastics are creeping into the boat building world, but necessarily in very few designs because of the colossal initial outlay required for tooling. ABS sheets are heated and vacuum formed over moulds; polypropylene is injection moulded. The advantage of injection moulding over vacuum moulding is that the material is not required to stretch around corners, at the very points of stress where strength is needed. The advantage of both plastics is their resistance to damage: they can be scratched but seldom broken, even after the

Ferro-cement construction. The steel rod reinforcing and layers of wire mesh ready for plastering with cement mortar.

most severe blow. And if they are scratched they need not be filled, for the material is uniform all the way through and impervious to water.

Steel and aluminium are used in the main for one-offs; steel is beloved of many world-girdlers for its strength in adversity; aluminium by offshore racers seeking lightness with strength.

Few professional boatbuilders use ferro-cement, which is a relatively inexpensive, quick and easy, though relatively heavy, form of construction and ideally suited to the amateur building of a large one-off. Steel rods follow the contours of the boat over a temporary framework. A skin is formed of wire mesh and the whole is plastered with cement in precisely the same way as the walls of a house.

Some ways with wood

Frames or ribs, known as steamed timbers (they are softened by steaming before being bent to shape) run

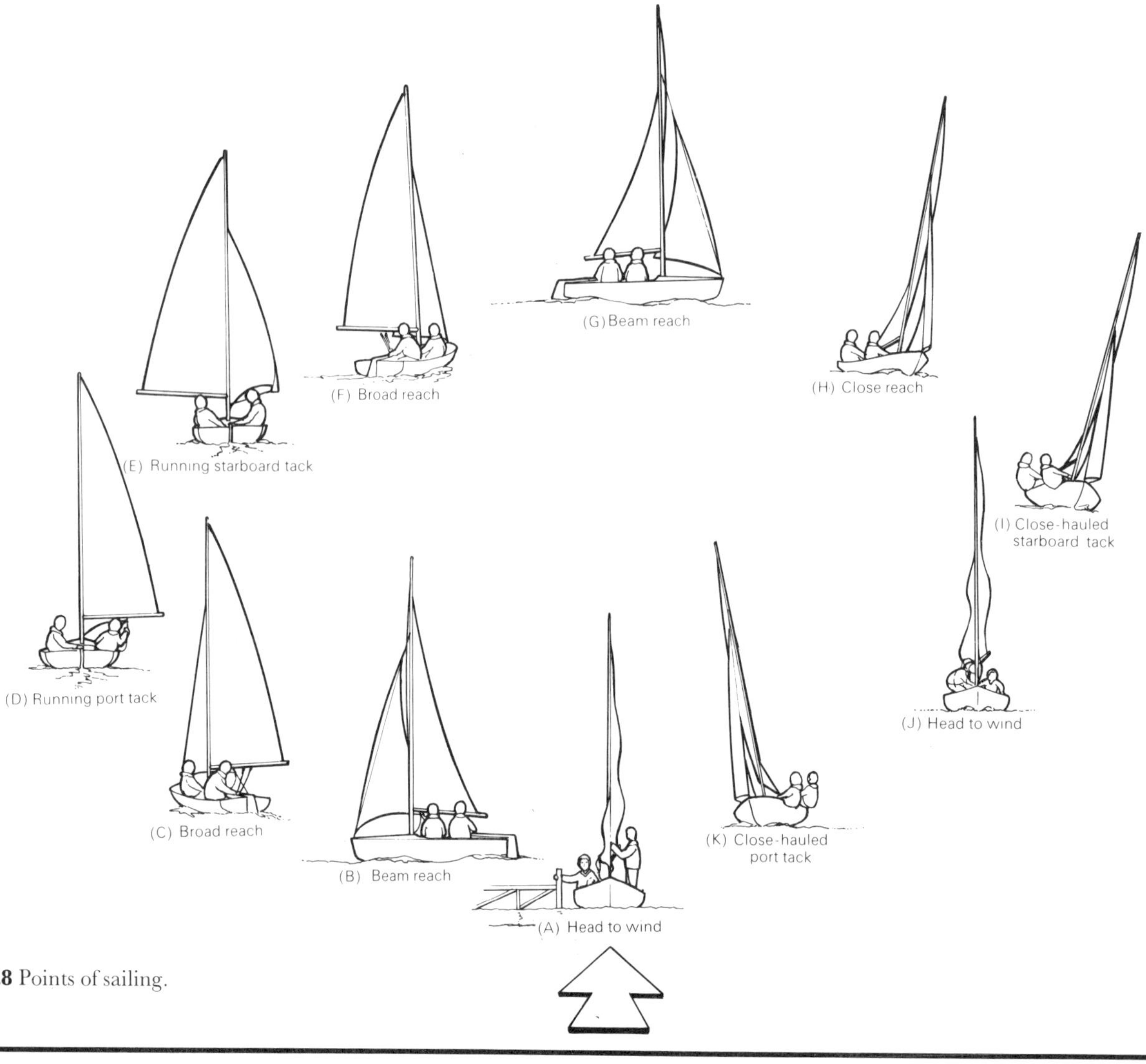

(G) Beam reach

(F) Broad reach

(H) Close reach

(E) Running starboard tack

(I) Close-hauled starboard tack

(D) Running port tack

(J) Head to wind

(C) Broad reach

(K) Close-hauled port tack

(B) Beam reach

(A) Head to wind

2.8 Points of sailing.

Snug in a mud berth. The planks of this clinker boat will not dry out and shrink and the mud will support her over the winter months.

across the hull and overlapping planks are fastened to these timbers in **clinker** construction. The fastenings used are copper nails which are clenched, or riveted, on the inside.

The modern way to produce a traditional-looking boat is to employ **glued clinker** construction. The overlapped planks are in fact of plywood and are glued where they overlap. Frames are not necessary because of the extra strength of the plywood.

In **carvel** construction the planks are arranged edge to edge and fastened to the steamed timbers to produce a smooth outer skin. Whereas the planks of a clinker boat overlap and, once they have taken up, butt together well along the overlap, it will be appreciated that planks laid edge to edge around the curve of a yacht's hull must necessarily meet only at their inner corner. The V-groove is filled by a method known as caulking, where lengths of cotton or oakum (rather hairy and string-like) are laid in the groove and the gap filled with a waterproof stopping compound such as putty. Modern caulking compounds tend to be synthetic and easily applied from a tube.

Strip planking could be said to be a modern variation on the carvel theme: planks are laid edge to edge around a framework – however, these planks are very small – their depth often no more than their

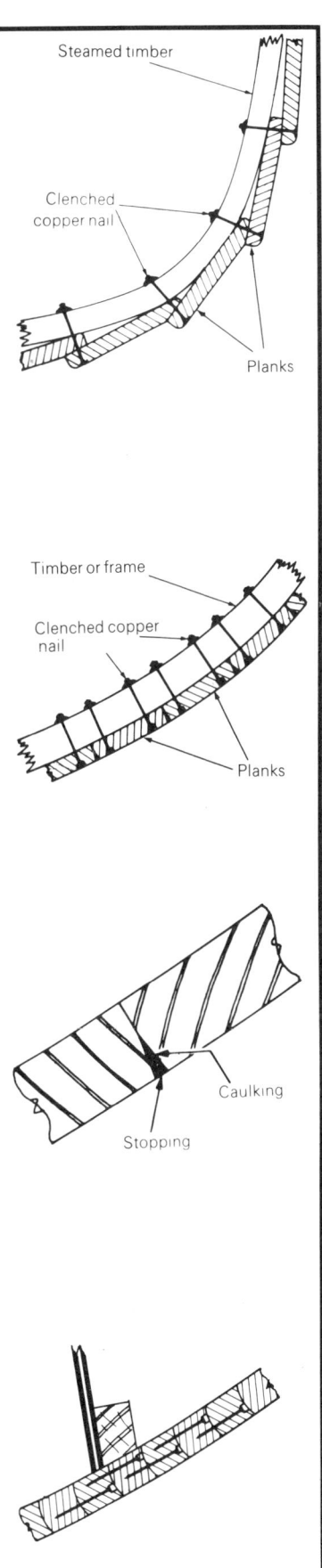

2.9a Clinker construction. The traditional method for boats up to about 20ft (6m) overall. Adjacent planks overlap throughout their length and are fastened with copper nails through steamed timbers.

2.9b Carvel construction. The planks lie edge-to-edge.

2.9c Carvel construction, seam detail.

2.9d Strip planking. A framework of bulkheads, transom, longitudinals and components such as bunk fronts is assembled and faired. The planks are nailed and glued both edge-to-edge and to the framework.

Carvel construction. *J. S. Biscoe*

Carvel construction, with main backbone set up. *Newmans*

Double diagonal construction. *Peter Cook*

Double chine plywood construction. *Smallcraft*

Cold moulded plywood construction. *Chippendale Boats*

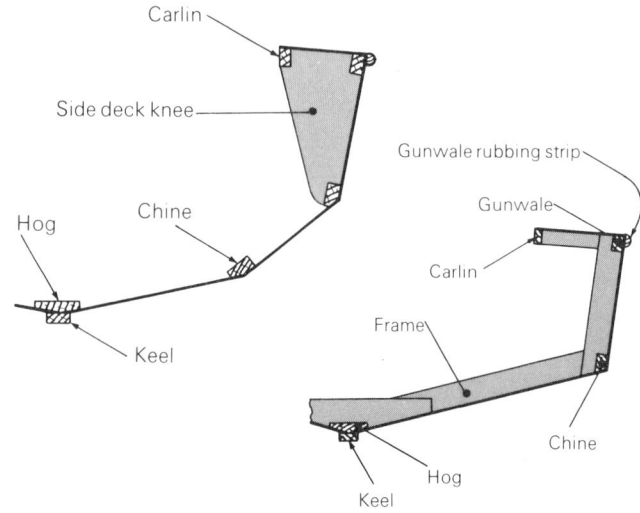

2.10 *(left)* Double-chine plywood construction.
(right) Hard-chine plywood construction.

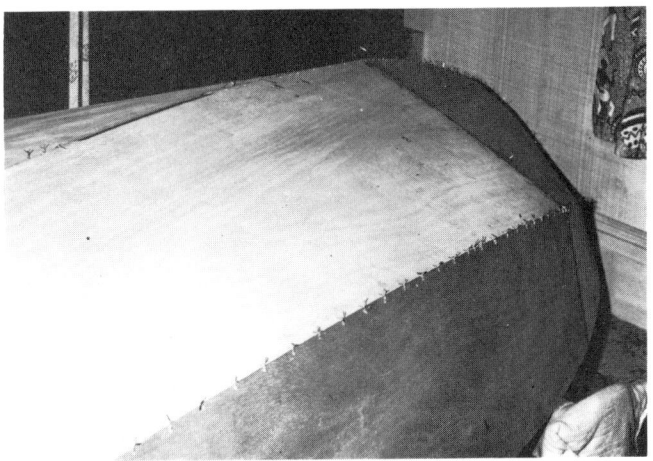

Stitch and glue construction. *Yachts & Yachting*

Seams taped with glassfibre and resin. *Yachts and Yachting*

Slot and tab construction: one step removed from stitch and glue and very, very easy.

Building a hard chine plywood dinghy over frames.

Stitch and glue construction: the hull panels are wired together and glassfibre tape applied over the joins.

A professional glassfibre boatbuilding production line.

thickness – and they are glued and nailed to each other as well as to the boat's frames. Caulking is unnecessary.

Double diagonal planking consists of two layers of planks, each laid diagonally to the keel but at right angles to each other. A third layer of planking, perhaps running fore and aft, may be laid over the first two layers to form **triple skin** construction.

The modern version of double diagonal planking is **moulded plywood** construction, where thin veneers of wood are glued on top of each other over a temporary mould, or framework. Staples are used to hold each layer in place until the glue sets and are removed before the next layer of veneer is glued on top.

Hard chine plywood construction is relatively simple, by virtue of the nature of the hard chine design itself. Flat plywood panels meet at a corner, or chine, where they are fastened to internal formers.

Stitch and glue is a development of hard chine construction for the home builder. With this method, pre-shaped hull panels are 'sewn' together with twists of copper wire and held together with glassfibre tape over the joins.

Slot and tab construction is stitch-and-glue taken on step further: pre-shaped panels are supplied, whose tabs locate in slots in other panels, in the manner of a cardboard cut-out on the back of a breakfast cereal packet. The inner seam of the join is glass-taped before the tabs are sawn off and tape applied to the outside, too.

Glassfibre

Preparation of a mould for a production run of glassfibre mouldings is a painstaking job. First a wooden plug must be constructed of the required shape – this in itself is work for a true craftsman because glassfibre is being used more and more for intricate shapes which do not lend themselves to ease of construction in wood. Then the plug must be faired in – smoothed down by the application of countless coats of filler paste interspersed by extensive rubbing down with abrasive paper until a completely dust-free, lump-free, ripple-free surface is achieved. Only then can the mould itself be laid up over the plug.

The lay-up of a glassfibre moulding, once the mould is ready for use, is quite simple. First the mould must be painted with a release agent – a moulding which fails to release can ruin the mould. Then the gel coat is painted on to the mould: this is the outer, pigmented, shiny layer of a glassfibre boat. If the gel coat colour is particularly deep or transparent some of the same pigment will be added to the resin when the first layer of glass fibres is applied. These may take the form of chopped strand mat or woven roving, a layer of which is laid on wet resin, then rolled or stippled until completely 'wetted-out' by the resin. Each layer of mat is left to harden before the next is applied. In areas of local stress, such as the areas behind fittings, an extra layer of glass mat will be applied.

Although primarily suited for production methods, it is possible for the home builder to produce a one-off in glassfibre. Some boatbuilders actually make their moulds available to the amateur and there are core materials which are suitable for bending over frames before being covered by glassfibre. Some foam is very suitable for this; in addition there is a product called C-Flex which incorporates glassfibre rods in a glassfibre mat. Because a mould is not used, a considerable amount of hand finishing is required by these methods to produce a perfect finish.

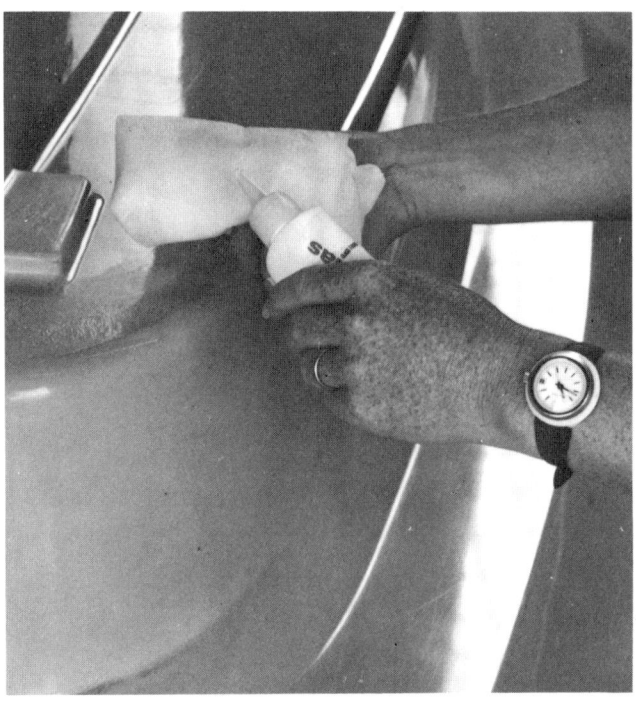

All my own work . . . from the application of the release agent to the moment of truth when the moulding is lifted from the mould. The Express Boating Organisation makes moulds of the Express Dinghy available to owners for amateur completion. And it really is quite easy. *Express Boating Organisation*

3 How everything fits together

A driver does not need to know what goes on under the bonnet of his car. A sailor, on the other hand, will be in a sorry plight if he does not understand the function of every fitting and every piece of rope on his boat.

In this chapter we shall concentrate on the simplest case: a sloop rigged dinghy equipped with basic fittings. This equipment becomes more complex and more robust in larger and more specialized boats.

Having said in Chapter 1 that our dinghy needs three things to turn it into a sailing dinghy (sails, centreboard, rudder) we now expand that number by two – for sails, unlike charmed Indian snakes, do not stand up by themselves. They need the support of a mast and, usually, a boom.

The traditional mast-making material, wood, has now almost universally given way to aluminium alloy which is extruded in tubes. A few manufacturers, mostly in Europe, persist with glassfibre masts but these are often heavy and are not generally popular.

The very basic mast is just a parallel-sided tube – maybe even two tubes which slot together in the middle for ease of stowage and transport. But this is anathema to the purist designer and racing man, who demands that his sails and his mast are matched closely, for perfect aerofoil characteristics. Most masts are tapered towards the top, partly to reduce excess weight aloft (there is less power in the top, narrow area of the sail) but often to allow the top of the mast to bend off in a controlled manner to reduce some of the power in the rig when a strong gust hits.

In racing dinghies the boom is often of a larger section than the mast for strength and lightness. It was once the fashion to use bendy booms but this has largely died out because of the necessity of matching the sail perfectly to the bend of the boom.

This is what happens to the mainsail when a boom vang is not used. Most of the wind is spilled as the sail twists away – although in these conditions, this crew is probably quite happy about that!
William G. Rowntree

The base, or heel, of the mast sits in a fitting called a mast step, sometimes on the foredeck, sometimes on the keel of the boat. The word 'keel' in this instance refers not to a fixed and ballasted appendage hanging

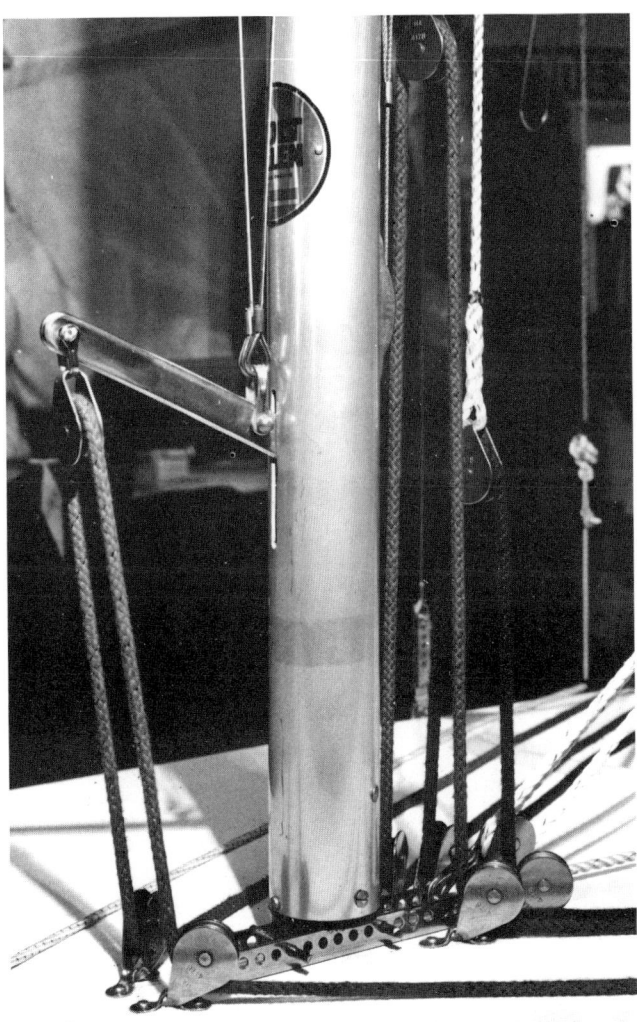

A fixed, deck-stepped mast on a Contender racing dinghy with a multiplicity of sail controls leading back to the helmsman.

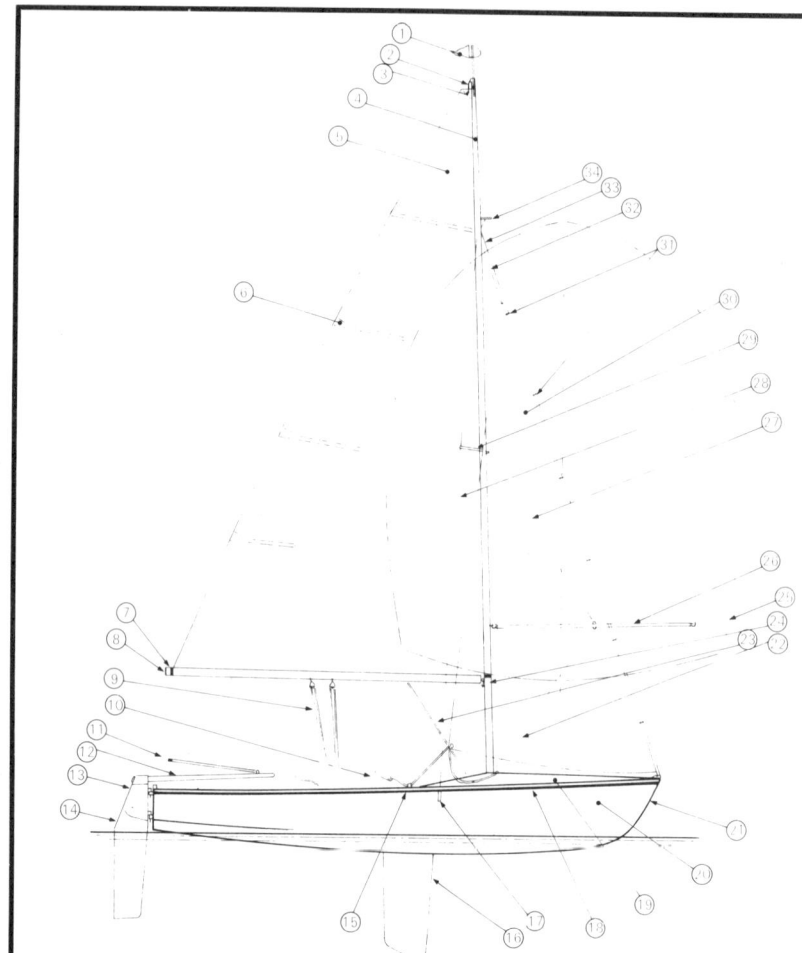

3.1 The parts of a sailing dinghy. 1 Burgee. 2 Main halyard. 3 Headboard. 4 Mast. 5 Mainsail. 6 Sail batten. 7 Boom black band. 8 Boom. 9 Mainsheet. 10 Headsail sheet. 11 Tiller extension (hiking stick). 12 Tiller. 13 Rudder stock. 14 Rudder blade. 15 Headsail sheet fairlead. 16 Centreboard. 17 Shroud plate. 18 Gunwale rubbing strip. 19 Foredeck. 20 Bow (starboard). 21 Stem. 22 Spinnaker pole downhaul. 23 Kicking strap (vang). 24 Gooseneck. 25 Spinnaker. 26 Spinnaker pole. 27 Spinnaker pole lift. 28 Shroud. 29 Spreader. 30 Headsail. 31 Headsail hanks. 32 Headsail halyard. 33 Forestay. 34 Spinnaker halyard crane.

This mast is keel stepped through a simple hole in the deck. The white bar is a chock which may be used to adjust the rake of the mast. *Jim Donaldson*

underneath the hull, but to the solid area of hull running fore and aft along the centreline. In wooden boats this is a thicker plank than those used in the hull itself. Often a deck-stepped mast will rotate to line up

with the boom and sail as the boat changes course, but this is not usually the case with keel-stepped masts.

The keel-stepped mast will probably have a second support at the point where it passes through the foredeck – the mast gate. A few single-sailed (una-rigged) boats use unstayed, cantilevered masts but boats with more than one sail need the extra support the control which rigging provides.

The mast is supported by rigging, usually of wire rope. The forestay attaches to the bow of the boat on the forestay fitting which will also have a take-off point for the foresail. The two side stays are called shrouds and are attached to shroud plates at or near the gunwale just aft of the mast. In a simple dinghy the shrouds and the forestay will be attached to the mast at the same height – this position is known as the hounds.

The simplest methods of attaching the boom to the mast are by means of jaws at the forward end of the boom or by a tongue on the boom which slots through a hole in the mast rather like a mortice and tenon joint. However, most boats utilize a gooseneck fitting, incorporating a type of universal joint if the mast does not rotate to line up with the boom.

The sail may be sleeved over the mast if the rig is unstayed, but it is more common to find that the luff of the mainsail is held captive in a track on the aft face of the mast – by means of a bolt rope attached to the sail or special sliders sewn to the luff of the sail.

The same system may be employed to attach the sail to the boom or the sail may be attached only at either end of the boom by its tack and clew, in which case it is said to be loose-footed.

The sails are hoisted by a halyard of wire or pre-stretched rope – commonly attached to an eye in the headboard of the sail by a shackle, then led round a sheave in the mast and back down the mast, either internally or externally to a cleat.

The tack of the mainsail may be pinned in position through a special tack fitting at the forward end of the boom or its position may be adjustable by means of a rope led through the tack eye to a cleat or tackle.

Similarly, the clew may be fixed or adjustable.

Very few sails are really triangular. If laid flat, with straight lines drawn to join each corner it will be seen that luff, leech and foot are all curved. The area of mainsail leech projecting beyond the straight line (its chord is called the roach) is often quite large, and would not stand unaided to follow the curve of the rest of the sail. Support is at hand in the form of sail battens, slender wands of wood or glassfibre which are fitted into batten pockets to encourage the roach area to assume the correct shape.

Some boats carry fully battened rigs, with battens which run the full depth of the sail. Correct adjustment of this type of battening can make or break a boat's performance.

The angle of the sails to the wind is controlled by sheets, predictably jib sheets and mainsheet. The jib

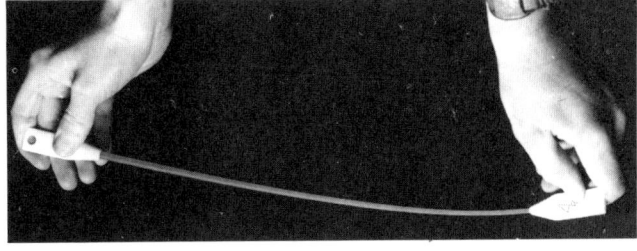

Aerofoil sail battens to help the leech of the sail to stand.

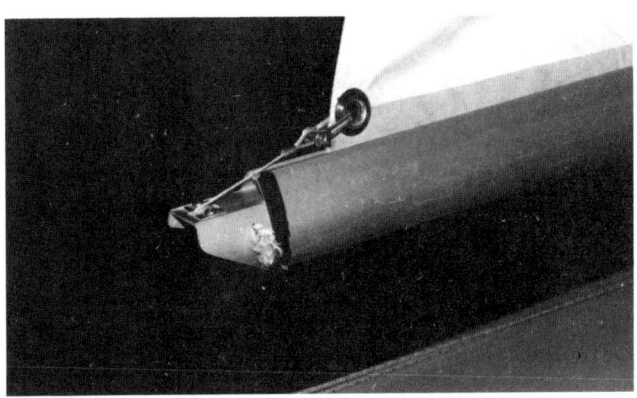

The clew may be tied to suit conditions, or be attached to an outhaul led forward along the boom to a cleat, to allow adjustment.

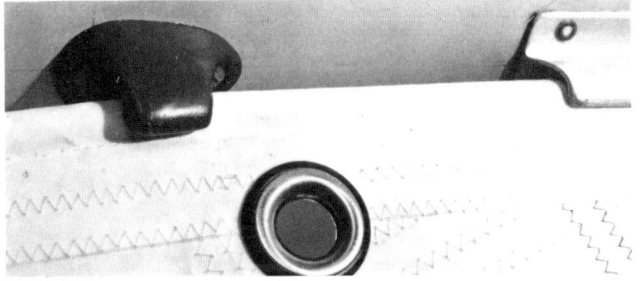

Detail of a luff groove and guide for the mainsail.

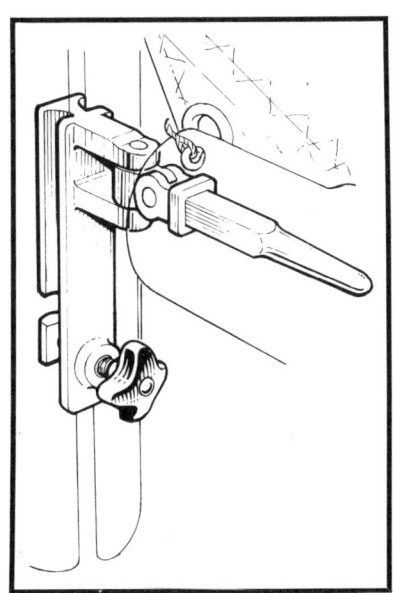

3.2 Sliding gooseneck on a dinghy.

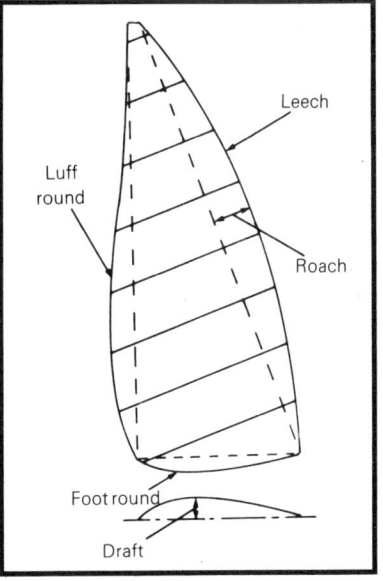

Leech

Luff round

Roach

Foot round

Draft

3.3 Because a sail has to set in a curve, the luff and foot will not lie in straight lines when the sail is spread out on the floor. Curvature in the sail is provided by shaping the edges of the individual clothes before they are stitched together.

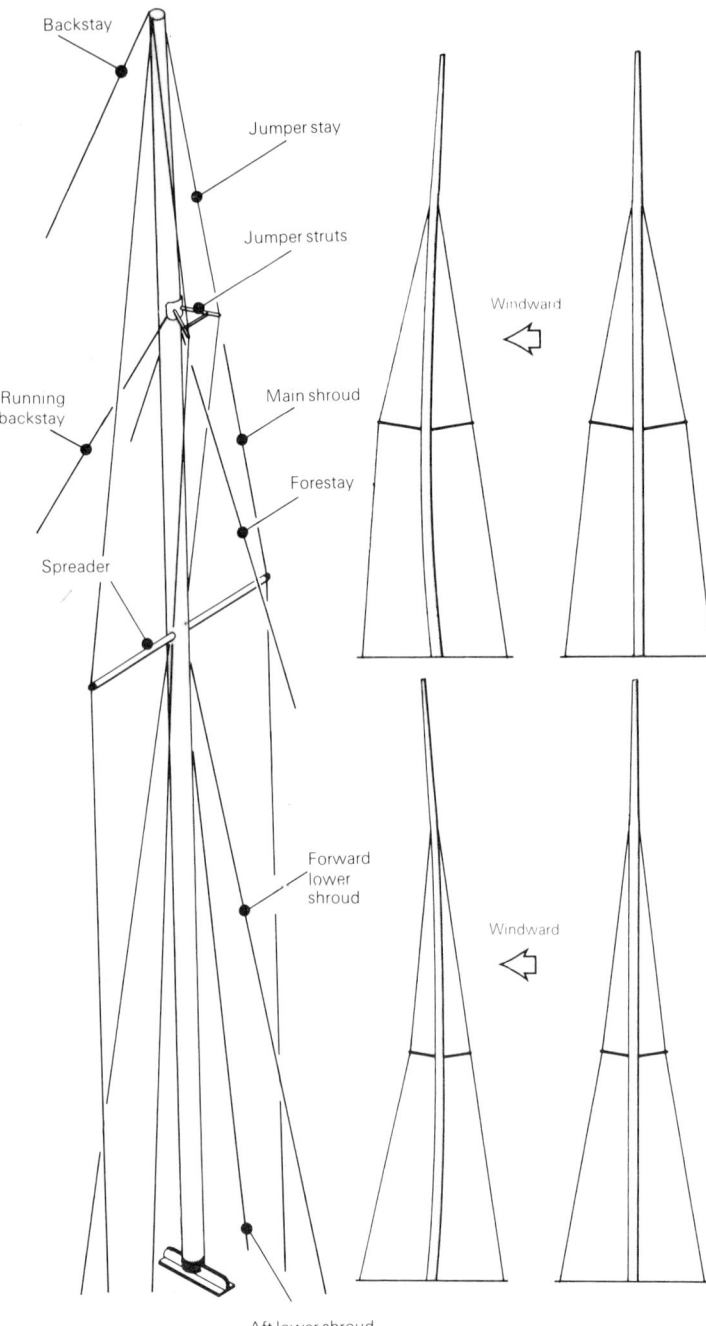

Backstay

Jumper stay

Jumper struts

Main shroud

Running
backstay

Forestay

Spreader

Forward
lower
shroud

Windward

Windward

Aft lower shroud

3·5 Spreader length. *(top right)* The spreaders are attached to the mast between the hounds and the deck and extend the shrouds. They act in conjunction with the shrouds either in compression or in tension to prevent or induce mast bend. Tension on the weather shroud will tend to bend the mast to windward at the top resulting in a stiff rig suitable for heavy crews. *(bottom right)* For light crews shorter spreaders are needed which cause the top of the mast to fall off to leeward when tension is applied to the weather shroud, thus spilling the wind from the mainsail.

sheets are attached to the clew eye of the jib and led one each side of the mast to a sheave, block or fairlead and cleat on the sidedeck. Mainsheet systems vary but will usually be a type of multi-whip purchase. A mainsheet fitted between the aft end of the boom and the transom of the boat utilizes the leverage of the whole length of the boom, and therefore requires fewer purchases than a centre mainsheet fitted between a take-off point near the middle of the boom and the centre thwart of the boat. Both types can be equally efficient: rigging the mainsheet depends largely on the helmsman's preference. A centre sheet, to a certain extent, balances the weight of the tiller whereas with an aft sheet the pull of both sheet and tiller is aft. When tacking with a centre sheet the helmsman must momentarily release his hold of the tiller, whereas with an aft system he simply tacks facing aft and changes hands on the sheet and tiller simultaneously.

The fall of the mainsheet should come to the hand from its lower take-off block. A mainsheet which is led to the hand from the boom is awkward in use.

The vertical angle of the boom, hence the twist in the mainsail, is controlled by the kicking strap or boom vang which may be a block-and-tackle purchase or may incorporate a winch or lever. The vang is rigged between a point well forward on the underside of the boom and the heel of the mast, or a strong point low in the boat just aft of the mast step. Its control line may be led to cleats on either sidedeck for ease of adjustment by the crew.

The spinnaker is stowed within the boat until needed, with the wind astern, either in a special spinnaker chute beneath the foredeck, in a bucket in the cockpit or in a spinnaker turtle (usually a fabric bag) hung on the pulpit of a keelboat. Ocean racers use all manner of special zipped socks and bags for hoisting, or may simply tie the sail in a lumpy sausage, using rotten cotton which breaks when the sail is hoisted and the sheets pulled hard.

The spinnaker, too, needs a boom, or pole, to control its angle to the wind and its height. The rules dictate that this pole must be carried on the opposite side of the boat to the main boom. The spinnaker sheets are usually attached in a small boat before launching so it remains only to clip on the halyard and hoist when the time comes.

The sheets are led to blocks at the gunwale of the boat, usually well aft, then back to blocks and cleats at the forward part of the cockpit within easy reach of the crew.

Just to confuse matters, the spinnaker sheet which is attached on the side of the spinnaker pole immediately becomes known as the guy; it is the guy which dictates the spinnaker's angle of attack to the wind. An

The smallest square-rigger of them all, the $7\frac{1}{2}$ft (2.3m) Optimist in which so many youngsters learn to sail. The loose-footed sprit sail teaches these budding world champions a very great deal about boat tuning for speed. *John Watney*

A classic picture of the Italian 'Mandrake' attired in matching spinnaker and big-boy, racing in the 1977 Admiral's Cup. *Silvio Mursia*

A Dutch Schouw, her mainsail reefed, makes the most of a spanking breeze on flat water.
John Watney

'It's all set, skip, now how about that beer?' Peter Poland's 'Matchless' competing in the 1975 Middle Sea Race in the Mediterranean. *Guido Alberto Rossi*

A good, workable dinghy layout. The mainsheet is transom mounted but the fall is led forward along the boom, then down to a final block and cleat on the centreline. The boom vang is part-wire, with a rope tackle for adjustment.

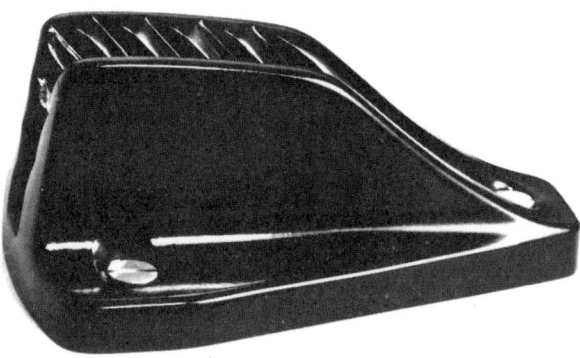

Two types of cleat: the cam cleat *(right)* whose jaws open to receive the rope, then clamp it tightly, and the Clam cleat *(left)* with no moving parts. The sides are ridged and tapered to hold the rope, which is released by a quick pull upwards and inwards.

On a three-sail reach, the slot between spinnaker and the fore and aft sails is just as important as the slot between the jib and mainsail. *Ken Fraser*

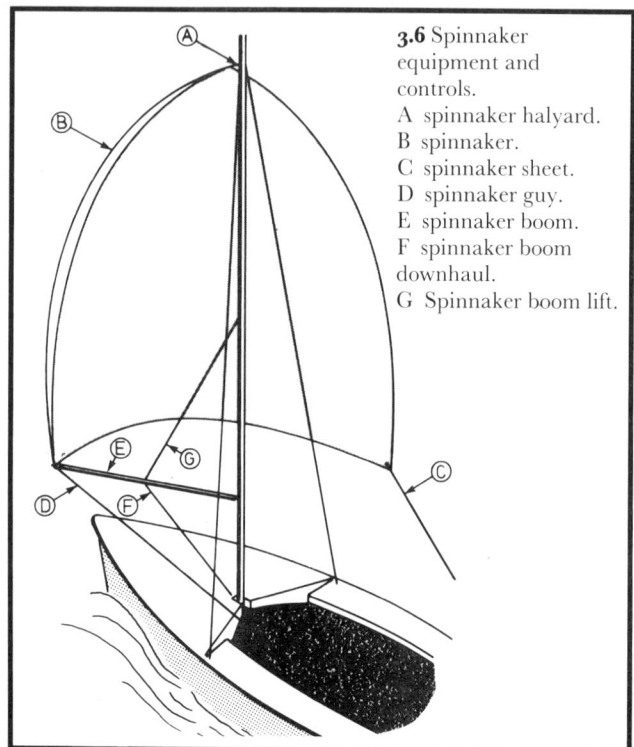

3.6 Spinnaker equipment and controls.
A spinnaker halyard.
B spinnaker.
C spinnaker sheet.
D spinnaker guy.
E spinnaker boom.
F spinnaker boom downhaul.
G Spinnaker boom lift.

Some larger boats hoist their spinnaker from a turtle, or cloth bag, which is hung on the pulpit. *Ajax Photo News*

uphaul/downhaul is attached to the mast and at the mid-point of the spinnaker boom to act in much the same way as the main boom vang. In its simplest form this may be a length of string with knots in, the knot at the correct height being caught behind an open cleat on the spinnaker pole.

Dinghies and some racing keelboats are kept on an even keel by the correct positioning of the crew's weight. In its basic form this involves the crew members sitting on or hanging over the sidedeck on the windward side of the boat to offset the weight of wind in the sails trying to capsize the boat to leeward. This would be a precarious occupation if it were not for the provision of toestraps (or hiking straps) – a length of terylene webbing of the type used for car and aeroplane seatbelts anchored fore and aft in the cockpit. These straps hold the crew's feet securely within the boat and are usually held just clear of the cockpit floor by a length of shockcord.

In classes which permit the use of a trapeze, the crew actually stands on the gunwale of the boat with his whole weight supported horizontally outboard by a wire led from the mast at or near the hounds fitting. At its lower end this wire is fitted with a ring which attaches to a substantial hook on the crew's trapeze harness and, a little higher up, a handle which the crew grabs as he moves in and out. A length of shockcord attached to the lower end of the trapeze wire is led through a fairlead on the gunwale, across the boat (neatly, via more fairleads), through a matching fairlead on the opposite gunwale and to the other trapeze wire. In this way the trapeze wires are automatically returned to their correct stowage position after use.

A few classes utilize a sliding seat, usually of plywood box construction, which slides in runners athwartships. The crew sits on the end of the plank with his feet braced against the gunwale – or curled round the plank itself if he has faith in his helmsman.

A dinghy rudder is hung on to the transom of the boat by pintles and gudgeons; a pintle being the pin-type fitting onto which is located the hole in the matching gudgeon. Conventionally the lower transom fitting and the upper rudder fitting are pintles but there is no hard and fast rule. The important point is that the fittings are of dissimilar lengths so that one may be located and the rudder pivoted on this until the other is aligned and the rudder may be dropped into position. The necessity of this is seldom appreciated until the day dawns when the rudder must be shipped at sea, when aligning both fittings at once is near-impossible.

A rudder may be fixed or lifting. The former is to be found at the extreme ends of the market: on the cheap and cheerful fun boats because it is inexpensive to produce; on the racing dinghies of purists because it may be constructed very lightly and it is important to keep unnecessary weight out of the ends of the boat. A lifting rudder blade pivots within the rudder cheeks and is more useful when launching or beaching in shallow water.

With a few exceptions, the rudder of a keelboat is permanently attached, either at the aft end of a full keel or separately beneath the aft end of the boat. Its stock – a tube or rod – passes through the hull and the tiller or wheel is fixed at the point where it emerges into the cockpit.

The tiller brings the control of the rudder within reach of the helmsman and a tiller extension can be

The transom of an Enterprise showing a lifting rudder. On the transom the lower rudder fitting is the pintle and the upper the gudgeon; on the rudder the reverse applies. The transom flap, made of clear acrylic sheet, can be opened to allow large quantities of water to drain out when the boat is swamped. The mainsheet block is attached to a slide running in a length of track the full width of the transom. *Peter Cook*

Detail of dinghy rudder and its hangings.

added to enable him to join his crew on the windward gunwale and still remain in command of his ship. The tiller extension must be capable of turning and pivoting without jamming and is therefore best attached by means of a special fitting incorporating a universal joint.

The dinghy is prevented from making excessive leeway by the presence of its centreboard or daggerboard. A centreboard pivots at its forward end and has the advantage of being easy to control. Its disadvantages are the length of the box required to house it within the cockpit, and the fact that when the centreboard is fully lowered the open box is a drag-producing, hence boat-slowing factor. A daggerboard slides vertically in a much smaller box and is removed when the boat is ashore. It has the advantage of simplicity but the disadvantage of less convenience in use, coupled with the possibility that, in its fully raised position, it may prevent the boom crossing the centre-line during a gybe.

4 The traditional scene

Picture a typical Saturday afternoon towards the end of the sailing season, on a popular part of the coast. The dinghies have had their fun and now sit on their trolleys in the dinghy park, the happy crews folding sails, tidying gear and climbing out of wet suits. Most of the modern family cruisers have found a berth in the local marina or picked up a spare mooring off the hard. A short offshore race is finishing: some of the bigger boats were in half-an-hour ago and now lie, packed away until the next race, between their mooring piles, made fast fore and aft; others have only just crossed the line, instantly to drop their sails, switch on the engine and motor in to the anchorage. A late finisher throws in a short, final tack to clear the committee vessel: yellow booted crewmen haul the genoa clew down to the footblock as winches ring, the sheet begins to creak as the winch is clicked-down a gear. The helmsman tucks himself to leeward of the huge, lightweight wheel, flicks his eyes up at the fluttering telltales on the genny luff and then concentrates on his instruments: apparent wind angle still a bit coarse, speed climbing nicely. The amplified boat speed indicator stirs into life again as the yacht gathers way after her tack, 6.12 knots is optimum speed for this sail and this wind speed, according to the sail-selection chart prepared from many weekends of sailing trials and previous races.

A little way away from all this feverish activity, the last fling of the afternoon before the still of evening, a small yacht with her sheets just eased heads for the entrance to a quiet creek largely ignored by the dinghy sailors (not enough open water for good racing) and rather too shallow and tortuous for the offshore racers. Unlike most of the racers and all of the modern family cruisers in the scene, our little yacht is not a masthead sloop – indeed she is not even a sloop and certainly her mast is not of alloy. Instead she is a gaff cutter. An elegant bowsprit carries her flying jib and her self-tackling staysail is set on a short boom, sheeted to a brass traveller (called a horse, as often as not) which

runs athwartships just forward of the mast. Her mainsail, tanned a russet brown as her other sails, swells aloft to a varnished gaff while two rows of bright white reef-points parallel to the boom contrast starkly with the soft brown of the sail. Her sheets are led not to multi-geared winches but through a series of varnished wood blocks before being turned-up on varnished oak staghorn cleats.

Her helmsman does not sail by instruments, but by the look of her sails and the fluttering of the burgee which flies from the truck of her white-painted topmast. As she runs into the mouth of the creek, he nods to the other member of the crew who lets go the staysail halyard, dropping the small, handy-size sail and quickly furling it on its boom. He pulls on a line running forward to a reel-drum at the tack of the jib and, as the helmsman casts off the sheet, that sail quickly rolls up around its own luff rope. As the little cutter's pace slackens, the crewman lets go one of the two halyards which take the gaff aloft and the peak of the mainsail drops until the gaff, which had been standing at an angle of about 60°, is horizontal and the mainsail scandalized. There has been no flogging of Terylene, no armies of men on the foredeck gathering in armfuls of sail, but on the cutter the power has been eased-off as gently as a careful pilot throttling back the engines of a giant passenger aircraft. With her main still aloft but only partly drawing, the little yacht rounds-up into the wind's eye and, as she loses way and begins to drop astern, her crewman lets go the anchor. With a rattle of chain her cable pays out, he drops a turn over the staunch oak samson post and the yacht snubs gently and lies safely to her anchor.

Later that evening, when the dinghy crews have showered and changed and drunk their beer and gone home, while the offshore men too have either headed for home or are sitting down to dinner in the yacht club, our friends on the little cutter are relaxing on board. The solid fuel bogey stove has been lit to combat the

Sun-dappled water and kindly light airs as a variety of traditional craft set off on a race organized by the British old Gaffers' Association. *Basil G. Emmerson*

chill of a seaborne evening, sometimes felt in summer, and the dishes from the evening meal have been cleared away. Where the modern family cruiser has her dinette, as comfortable as the buffet car in a second class railway carriage, and the modern ocean racer has nothing at all, save the john and seventeen sails, our cutter is quite a little home. Two long settee berths flank the cabin, on which our two friends now recline, backs propped against the bulkhead and a strategically placed cushion or two completing the pose of idle comfort. The wings of the saloon table have been folded down to leave only a narrow central rail, wide enough to take a bottle and a glass or two but not so wide as to block the cabin sole completely. As night draws in, the owner goes on deck to hoist the kerosene-fed anchor lamp, while below the polished brass oil lamps in the cabin bathe the mellow woodwork in a golden glow and cast warm, dark shadows behind the beams across the deckhead. The owner comes below, passes a remark about the weather and the prospects for tomorrow's sail and goes back to

his comfortable perch. There is a clink of bottle-neck on glassrim and our two friends enjoy a traditional end to a day's cruising on a traditional yacht.

The origins of sailing craft

Since some unknown early Egyptian mariner first set a reed sail to save the effort of paddling his reed boat downwind, the wind has been a traditional source of power for seafaring man. Pictures from Archaic Egypt believed to be at least 6,000 years old show craft with recognizable sails, and it is interesting to note that such paintings appear alongside pictures of oared craft. These are the oldest known pictures of actual boats and indicate that the development of the oar and that of the sail were coincidental. It was probably the Phoenecians, trading the Mediterranean and beyond in the days before the might of the Roman empire had razed Carthage to the ground, who had the first ocean-going ships and who were the first to use the wind for long journeys, but throughout the period of classical history the sail and the oar were complementary, the latter the vessel's main power source, the former used when the wind set fair and there was no difficult manœuvring to be done. Somewhere in the Mediterranean, probably on smaller coastal craft which could not wait for days for a fair breeze and which did not have large crews to propel them against contrary winds, the square sail, useful only for sailing downwind, developed into the lateen sail, which can be trimmed to allow the vessel to make to windward. Certainly by the twelfth century, lateen sails were considered old in the Mediterranean, and when in 1492 Columbus set sail with the 'Pinta', the 'Nina' and the 'Santa Maria', his favourite vessel, the 'Nina', was rigged as a lateen caravel. (She was re-rigged with square sails, to match the others, in the Canary Islands later in the voyage).

The fore-and-aft sail as we know it probably developed from the lateen, certainly on small craft used for fishing, coasting and longshoreing. Unfortunately such humble craft rarely attracted the interest of draughtsmen and it is not until the end of the fifteenth century that we have pictures of craft rigged in a manner which might seem familiar to the yachtsman of today.

Much has been written about the introduction of yachting: the word probably derives from the Dutch word *yaght*, meaning swift, and applied to anything from ships to hunting dogs. The use of such vessels purely for pleasure was started (at least so popular history now records it) by the English King Charles II, who was presented with such a vessel by the city of Amsterdam in 1660. Pleasure sailing in the modern sense only began to gather momentum at the end of the nineteenth century and, although doubtless men and women who lived by the sea had taken to the water on a pleasant day as a relaxation for years before then, it is – not surprisingly – those educated men with a fair amount of leisure who published books about their pastime who are now remembered as the pioneers of sailing for pleasure.

By its very nature, the traditional scene has had more to do with cruising and going to sea for its own sake than with racing, where often it is that which is most radical which does best. So these amateur seamen, as they called themselves (to some, the very word yachtsman was anathema) modelled themselves on the professional coastwise seamen, the fishermen, smacksmen and bargemen, of the day and likewise their craft. Yachts – seagoing yachts particularly – were modelled on the rugged working craft which, with the advent of steampowered vessels, were fast becoming the last stronghold of sail. Gradually in the commercial world where efficiency is all, steam and the internal com-

The square rig nowadays tends to be restricted to training ships, and the occasional ocean cruiser used in trade-wind work. *Yachts & Yachting*

bustion engine ousted sail, and it was left to the sport of yachting to develop the sailing craft. It is a curious fact that greater advances in the design of efficient sailing craft have been made in the past 75 years, when sailing for pleasure has been the driving force behind design change, than in many centuries of commercial sail. The merchantmen of the middle ages seem less different from the merchantmen of the Romans, and the warships of Nelson's fleet less different from the galleons of the Spanish Main, than does the ocean racer of today when compared with the schooner 'America' or the racing yachts of even fifty years ago.

But while yacht racing forged ahead in the matter of development and design, there were those who prefered their sailing craft to be as they had always been. Thus what began as imitation of the best and most efficient craft available became the preservation of a dying type of sailing craft and indeed what might be regarded as a dying art – that of the traditional seaman under sail.

The spectrum of the traditional scene today ranges

from those who painstakingly seek out and restore to life old working craft, such as the fishing smacks of the east and south coasts of Britain, the spritsail-rigged sailing barges of the Thames Estuary or the working craft of the eastern seaboard of the United States, to those who buy and sail modern replicas of old-time craft: in America the replicas of the Friendship sloops or the Catboats of New Jersey and Massachusetts and the coast between; in Britain the Cornish Crabber or the modern gaff cutters built by small yards specializing in such craft. Between these two lies every shade of commitment to the preservation of the traditional style of small boat sailing, from those who find and restore sixty- and hundred-year-old yachts, and those who would be seen dead before they would allow a swaged-end wire splice or plastic-and-nylon block aboard, to those who are happy to accept the convenience which modern materials such as glassfibre and alloy can bring but who nonetheless enjoy the added interest which can accrue by doing things – be it splicing their own rope or wire or exploring the one-time haunts of the working sailing craft – in a traditional manner.

Traditional construction methods

Wood is the traditional material for the construction of small craft the world over, and naturally is regarded as the traditional material for yacht construction. Indeed, it is difficult to see how a yacht built of any other material can be regarded as being in the traditional vein although there are a number of series-produced reproduction craft on the market both in Europe and America built of other materials, usually glassfibre. Traditional sailors most normally eschew such modern materials, just as they prefer to have a brass-bound cedar or galvanized metal bucket aboard, rather than a plastic pail. Many traditional small-boat sailors feign a hearty dislike for yachting modernity, a dislike which is sometimes more pretended than real but which sometimes, true enough, is genuinely felt.

The yacht built in the traditional manner owes her form and construction to practices developed over many centuries of shipbuilding and her construction resembles that of a living creature, with backbone, skeleton of major and minor bones and a skin of planking.

The keel is the backbone, the inverted ribcage of her timbers her main bones. The keel lays the foundation for the hull's longitudinal strength, the timbers give her her athwartships strength. Then the stringers, the fore-and-aft lighter bones, are laid over the timbers to spread upwards and outwards the strength imparted by the keel. (See the photographs of carvel construction on page 28).

Although bermudan rigged, the jib-topsail cutter 'Zelia' is every inch a traditional cruiser as she scurries along with her dinghy following faithfully astern at the end of its painter. *Janet Harber*

Around the upper edge of the timbers runs a massive structural member called the beam shelf, and to this are laid and attached the deckbeams which run athwartships from timberhead to timberhead, one beam to each pair of timbers, tying the ship's sides together. Down the centre of the emerging deck, the kingplank joins stemhead to sternpost, its continuous run broken by the interruption of cabin and cockpit. Were we building the yacht purely for strength, there would be no interruption to the kingplank, and no apertures in the deck, but of course only in a model yacht could we do that, since the point of the exercise is to have a craft in which people may go to sea, and people must have some way of getting inside. So where we have to break the line of the kingplank and deckbeams for hatches, cockpit, cabin and so on, great care must be taken not to weaken the overall structure.

The deckbeams immediately fore and aft of the opening are strengthened, either by increasing the size of timber of which they are made or by doubling –

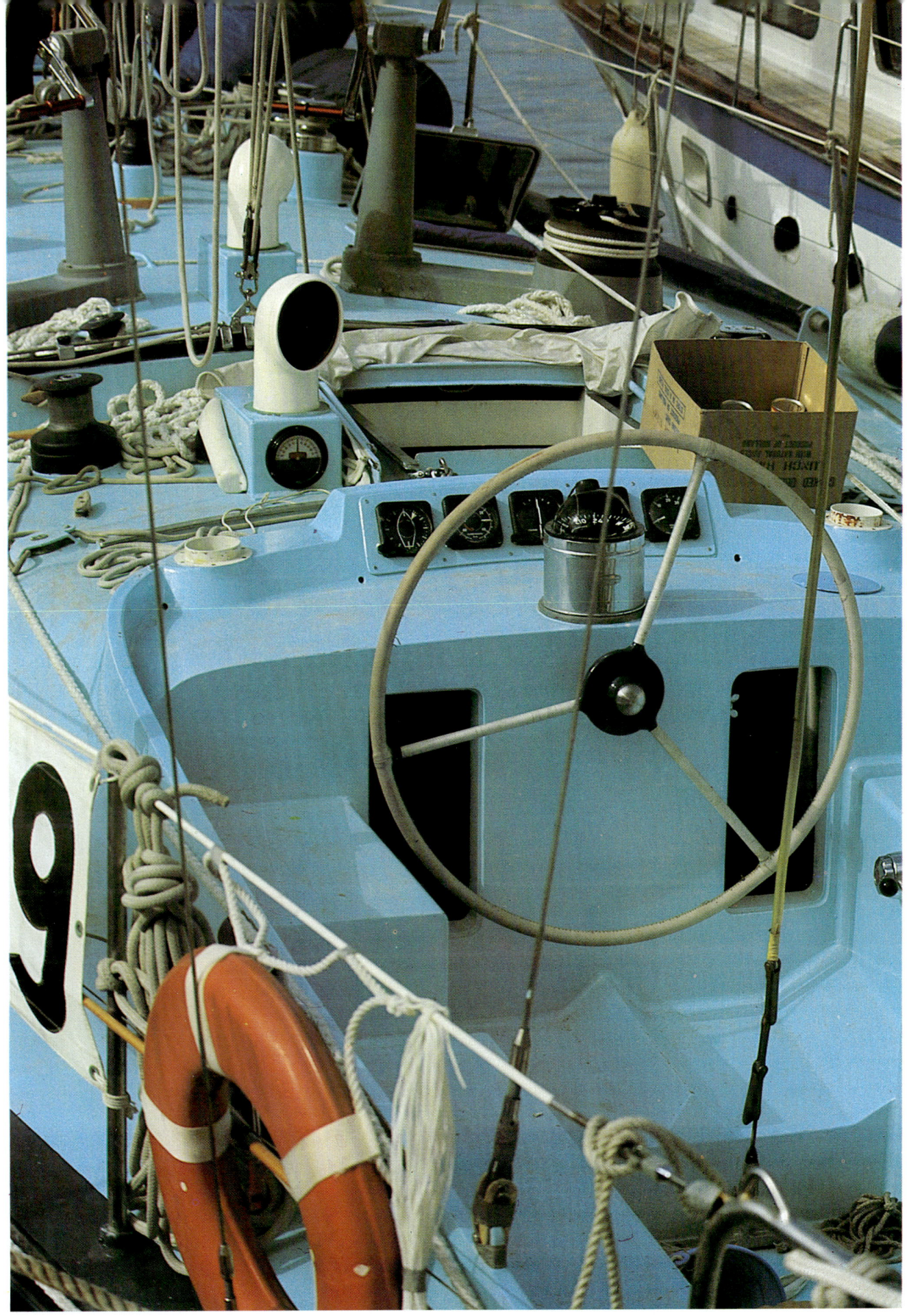

The small helmsman's cockpit of 'Enteara'. Crew's access to the cabin is via the small deck hatch just forward of the wheel. *Guido Alberto Rossi*

A gentle cruise under the shadow of Scotland's highest mountain range; this is the Rival 34ft (10.36m) 'Seòl Alba'. *John Watney*

Italy's 'Vihuela' has a tiny advantage over Germany's 'Pinta' in an Admiral's Cup inshore race of 1975. *John Watney*.

The modern offshore racer with its masthead rig and huge downwind sails makes the South Coast
One Design look almost old fashioned by comparison. The SCOD is still raced keenly from
Cowes and may almost be said to be England's precursor of the modern concept of the Offshore
One-Design. *John Watney*

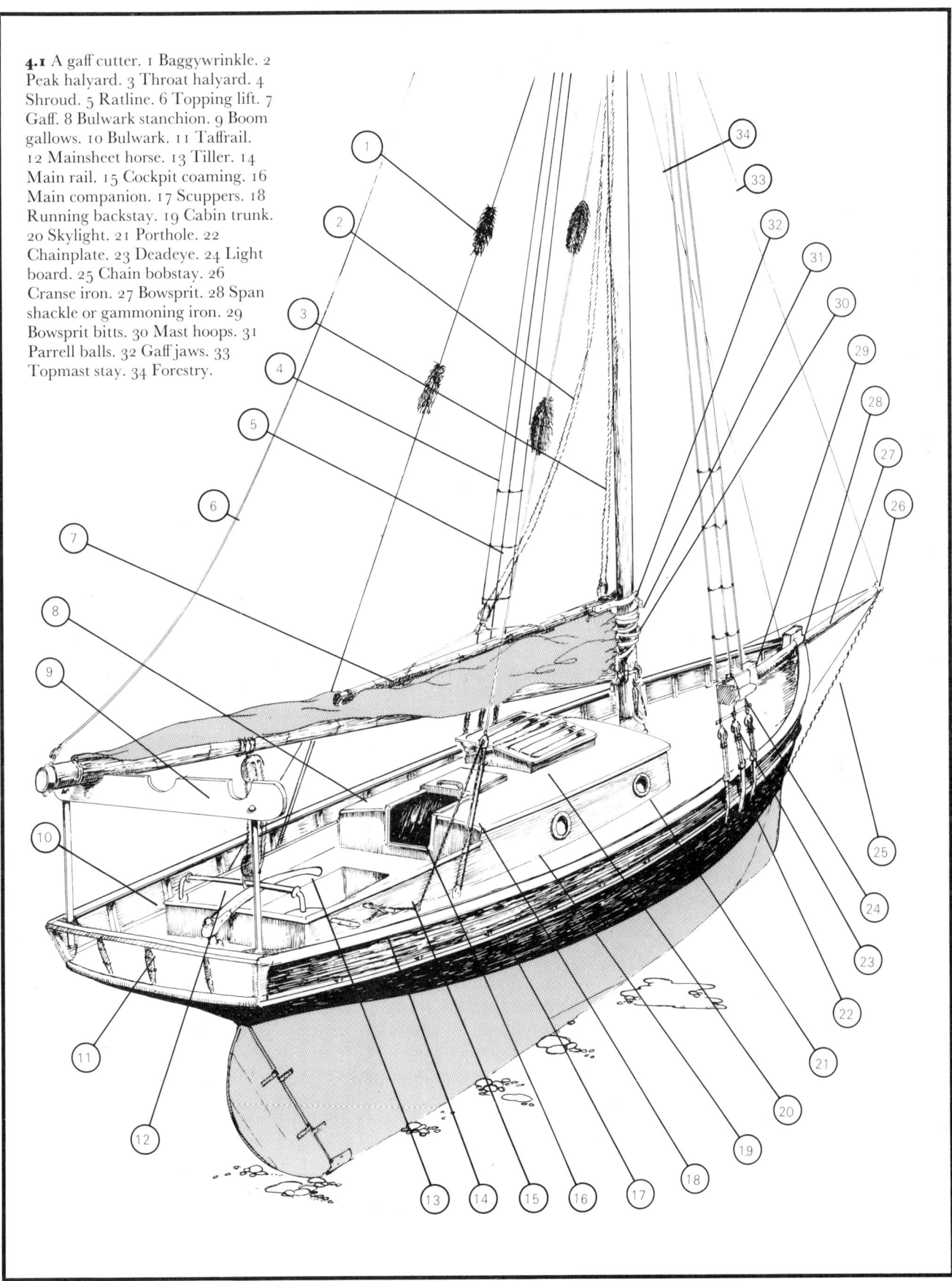

4.1 A gaff cutter. 1 Baggywrinkle. 2 Peak halyard. 3 Throat halyard. 4 Shroud. 5 Ratline. 6 Topping lift. 7 Gaff. 8 Bulwark stanchion. 9 Boom gallows. 10 Bulwark. 11 Taffrail. 12 Mainsheet horse. 13 Tiller. 14 Main rail. 15 Cockpit coaming. 16 Main companion. 17 Scuppers. 18 Running backstay. 19 Cabin trunk. 20 Skylight. 21 Porthole. 22 Chainplate. 23 Deadeye. 24 Light board. 25 Chain bobstay. 26 Cranse iron. 27 Bowsprit. 28 Span shackle or gammoning iron. 29 Bowsprit bits. 30 Mast hoops. 31 Parrell balls. 32 Gaff jaws. 33 Topmast stay. 34 Forestry.

placing two ordinary beams together to make one of greater strength. Where the beams which would otherwise run across the ship have to be cut to make the opening their ends are joined by a fore-and-aft beam called a carlin, and gradually the framework of the yacht takes recognizable shape. Everywhere attention is paid to giving her strength: to reinforce each joint, floors, knees and aprons are used where timbers join the keel, where beams join timbers and where stringers join the stemhead.

Finally, the skeleton of the yacht is complete, needing only its skin planking. Each fore-and-aft run of planking is called a strake and, starting nearest the keel with the garboard strake, the planking is laid over the bones of the framework, port and starboard sides being brought along together so as not to load the framework unfairly and induce an irredeemable twist to the entire structure of the yacht. Traditionally, the planking is fastened to the framework by an age-old form of riveting using copper nails and rooves. The nail is square in section, and is driven through a pre-drilled hole in plank and timber. The roove, a dome-shaped washer, is slipped over the inner end of the nail as it emerges through the timber and the nail end, carefully snipped to length, is tapped-down over the roove to make a tight fastening, the nailhead holding the planking on the outside and the roove preventing the fastening from pulling out. It is a task which requires skill from the two men (or more traditionally, the boatbuilder and his apprentice) to do the job neatly and to finish each fastening so that all have the same degree of tightness. Badly done, the rooves appear untidy, some heavily flattened against the timber and some barely changed from their original dome shape, but worse than the unsightly appearance is the fact that some fastenings are tighter than others, thus are taking an unfair part of the load and an unfair strain. The planking is held on, then, by only a few of the fastenings, instead of by all: a sure recipe for trouble in the future.

Copper fastening is a mode of construction seen less and less, even in otherwise traditionally-built craft. It is time consuming and labour-intensive, and the fastenings themselves are expensive, partly because of the price of copper and partly because of the fall in demand which has led to their being more expensive, individually, to make. Many wood craft, traditional in other respects, are now fastened by the glued-and-screwed method. As the highly descriptive name implies, the joint is made by using special waterproof glues (traditionally made from recipes involving such choice ingredients as gypsum and horses' hooves, but now most often entirely synthetic glues of a strength which the boatbuilder of even thirty years ago would have found incredible) and by using wood screws (brass

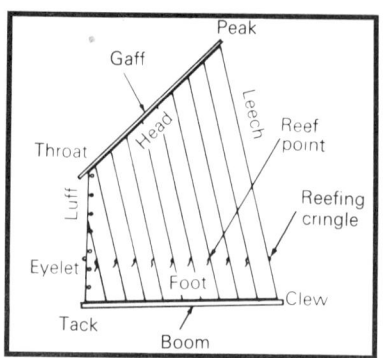

4.2 The parts of a gaff sail.

or better still phosphor bronze) to hold the pieces together until the glue has cured. (Incidentally, glue is not normally used on the planks of a traditionally planked-up boat in case a strake has at some later stage to be replaced.)

Another traditional method of fastening sometimes still seen, especially on smaller craft, is clench-fastening. Here, only the nail is used, driven in against a hard surface – such as the face of a hammer – so that the inner end is turned down and then tapped-down firmly against the face of the timber. This somewhat crude-but-effective method was common in the building of working boats, and is often to be seen on older yachts built by yards which combined both activities, rather than specializing purely in the rather finer skills of yacht-building. Although copper is most usually the material of which traditional fastenings are made, iron is not uncommon. Traditionally-constructed commercial fishing boats, planked of larch on oak timbers and iron fastened, are still built by yards who occasionally receive an order for a sturdy cruising yacht.

No definite rules can be laid down regarding the shape of the traditional yacht, although the differences in her general appearance when compared to the product of modern yacht-building methods would strike all but the most uninterested observer. By the nature of the development of yachting, and yacht cruising in particular, the shape of yachts built in the first half of this century was dictated to a great extent by the shape of the commercial working craft still eking-out a living under sail. Bold, straight stems, proud bowsprits, pronounced sheer and low, sweeping counters came from fishing smacks which needed high bows to meet the conditions which might arise to challenge a craft forced to spend foul weather as well as fair at sea; the bold sheer came likewise, and the low counter and broad decks aft were the legacy of the craft's principal purpose as a sea-borne working platform: hauling nets or oyster dredges is a good deal easier over a low stern than over a towering topside. Other craft offered other qualities, other shapes. A classic example is the so-called Colin Archer type, a full-bodied, deep-keel double-ended craft of massive construction and proportions with a relatively snug rig. These much-loved cruising yachts are based on the sailing Norwegian lifeboats which once accompanied the fishing fleets off the western coast of Scandinavia, down into the North Sea, far out into the North Atlantic or high into the Arctic. The craft were designed by the Scottish-Norwegian naval architect Colin Archer to keep the sea in all weathers, safe as the House Built Upon Rock, to succour the fleet in times of stress – which would usually be when the weather was at its worst. Their sea-keeping qualities have been treasured by generations of tradition-loving yachtsmen looking for a good cruising boat – but forgeting, perhaps, that the originals were designed for the express purpose of spending a long time in the one place: not always the aim of the cruising yachtsman.

The gaff-rigged yacht

Perhaps the most singular aspect of the traditional yacht, setting her apart from her modern sister and uniting the most divergent of traditional hull shapes, is the rig: almost universally, traditional yachts are gaff-rigged. Indeed there are those who would say that, by definition, a sailing yacht rigged with the bermudan rig (originally called the Marconi rig when it first appeared in yachting, because of its likeness to the then-new radio masts of Mr Marconi) is not traditionally rigged and is therefore not a traditional yacht. We will not take quite so exclusive a view, for there are plenty of yachts with triangular (as opposed to the quadrilateral of the true gaff rig) mainsails which are otherwise as traditional as holly at Christmas, but it is true that the gaff mainsail may be regarded as more the badge of the traditional yacht as may any other single item or feature.

Gaff rig is the direct descendant of the square sail of the Phoenicians and the Vikings, and of all the rig variations and varieties which yachting has spawned from those distant ancestors, the gaff cutter must be regarded as the purest of line. In modern parlance a cutter is a single-masted sailing craft with more than one sail ahead of the mast (hence the term headsail). That, it must be emphasized, is but a modern yachtsman's somewhat pedantic definition, for in the days of sail a cutter was any handy, easily manoeuvred small craft used for general duties about the fleet or harbour or for stealthy work against an enemy: it is easy to see why the name should have crept at an early stage into the vocabulary of yachting, for it was from such craft that the first yachts took their inspiration.

The cutter rig, as we know it, was already popular in coastal working craft – those which had to go both against and with the wind – when it was adopted by yachtsmen, and the reason is plain to see. Before the days of powerful winches and strain-conquering hydraulics there was a natural limit to the size of small boat sails: that which could be handled easily by one man. The mainsail, constrained on three of its four sides by spars – gaff, mast and boom – and controlled by a multi-part purchase was one solution, but there was room on board most small craft for only one such sail. Other sails, set on the stays which support the mast fore-and-aft (and hence termed staysails) had to be sufficiently small to be trimmed by the short-handed crew without mechanical aids. A number of small sails, rather than a single big headsail, was the obvious answer.

In yachting terms there was also the problem that until very recently, until the development of modern synthetic sailcloths especially, making large headsails which would keep their shape – and be sufficiently controllable in the matter of shape when set – was particularly difficult.

Even today, the cutter rig has many advantages over the all-pervading masthead sloop rig for the small family cruiser, advantages which are well-realized by those who own traditionally-rigged yachts. The two headsails, as well as being individually more easily handled than the single genoa, are a good deal more versatile. The modern deck-sweeping genoa becomes inefficient as the sheet is eased and a course shaped across the wind, and must ideally be replaced by a high-clewed reaching headsail: all very well for the racing yacht with plenty of crew and a plethora of sails in the fo'c's'le from which to choose, but less happy for the family out for a gentle sail. The cutter, with her high-cut jib set flying to the end of her bowsprit (its tack is run out from on-deck by a traveller ring rigged round the bowsprit and pulled in and out by a control line) and her lower-cut boomed staysail, knows no such problem and enjoys a happy advantage when the sheets are just eased. As the wind pipes-up, the sloop must suffer a series of headsail changes as large genoa is replaced by number two genoa, in turn to be replaced by working jib and then storm jib. On the simple cutter, however, the headsails are either up or down: first the jib is handed, leaving only the staysail (which, easily controlled on its own little boom, really comes into its own as the breeze freshens) and then the staysail may be reefed from the relative security of the foredeck near the mast. Only in the worst of weather is the storm canvas bent-on.

One sail beloved of traditionalists is the topsail, which is non-existent in the bermuda rig, being impossible to set. The topsail fills the gap normally left between gaff and topmast (that part of the mast above the jaws of the gaff when the mainsail is fully set) and is a most useful sail, especially on the wind where it increases the effective luff-length of the mainsail, an important element in windward performance. There are two basic types of topsail, the jib-headed and the jackyard. The jib-headed topsail is carried without any spars of its own and its head is hoisted direct to the masthead of the yacht while the jackyard topsail, lofty aristocrat of the traditional rig, is sent aloft on its own luff-spar, the jackyard of the name. The topsail halyard carries the jackyard to lie alongside the mast, but extending skywards above it to enable a much bigger and more effective topsail to be set. To the traditional heart, there are few sights more noble than a graceful jackyard cutter working out in a good breeze.

This, then, is a brief look into the world of the traditionalist in sailing. Perhaps in forty years' time there will be those who will maintain and preserve the Ton Cuppers of today, scouring the junkyards and second-hand chandlery shops for parts for a three-speed winch, or spending a fortune to try and keep a genuine late-70's amplified boat speed meter working. Today such exotica has no part in the traditional scene, but already other materials and gear, which once might have sent a shudder down the spine of any self-respecting lover of traditional boats, are in common use. Those russet-brown sails we watched disappearing into the mouth of the creek at the beginning of the chapter were in all probability Terylene; a good deal easier to find now than Egyptian cotton or Admiralty Flax Number Two, and a good deal cheaper, to boot. The cordage on board would almost certainly have been synthetic, for natural fibre rope has all but disappeared from the shelves of even the most traditional chandlery, where plastic wrappers and pre-packed everything has replaced the pungent tang of tarred hemp which once quickened the blood of every customer as he walked in the door.

On the credit side, more and more yachtsmen are discovering that keeping and running an older boat can be highly rewarding and – quite simply – great fun. The traditionalists are clearly here to stay.

5 Dinghies

Centreboard dinghies can be sub-classified into general purpose dayboats and racing boats. Dayboats are dinghies for relaxed sailing and are designed more for comfort than for speed, having a relatively small sail area. They are a comparatively slow and stable type, make less physical demands on the crew than the racing dinghy and are suitable for novices because they call for slower reactions than do more high-powered designs. They are also ideal for those who want to sail purely for the pleasure of sailing, for whom speed is not the ultimate objective.

It is easy to conjure up a picture of a racing dinghy flying along in a welter of spray, crew out on the trapeze and fighting an enormous spinnaker with all his might. But a racing dinghy is for the most part a dinghy which is raced and therefore some dayboats are included in this category. The breed starts at the bottom end of the size scale with the little Optimist, all $7\frac{1}{2}$ft (2.3m) of it, and finishes somewhere around the Olympic Flying Dutchman at nearly 20ft (6m). In between there is seemingly a class for everyone – and his brother – but that is no deterrent to a new design taking the world by storm every now and then. Many of the simpler racing dinghies are also used for day sailing and are therefore quite suitable for beginners, whereas the out-and-out racing dinghy which carries a large sail area, and probably a trapeze, is more suitable for skilled sailors who want the stimulus of competition and physical exertion, and who are prepared to sacrifice comfort and stability for speed.

General Purpose Dinghies

It is the general purpose dinghy which so often gives the novice his first taste of the sea – and on his choice of boat rests the future of his sailing career. A wrong first choice can so easily lead to disillusionment with the sport as a whole.

The minimum practical length for a small sailing dinghy is about 8ft (2.5m) but a boat of this size must realistically be considered a child's boat or a very short-distance fun machine. A small boat like this will not possess a good turn of speed and, although this in itself may not appear to be important, it can lead to some potentially dangerous situations in a seaway if the boat is unable to outpace the tidal stream. A 7ft-8ft (2m-2.5m) yacht tender with a makeshift rig can provide a lot of fun in the moorings when the parent craft is anchored for the night, but a small dinghy should

A tender with a sail can be a lot of fun among the moorings when the parent craft is anchored for the night.

Basic, beamy, roomy and stable. A useful family day sailer of
around 12ft (3.6m). *Anthony J. Linton*

always be used with the utmost care, close to the shore
and, if in the hands of children, under experienced
supervision.

A dinghy of 11ft (3.4m) or so is more versatile. It is
still light enough to be carried on a car roofrack, large
enough to carry two or even three adults, has more
stowage space and the potential to carry a larger, more
powerful rig which will give better performance under
sail.

Over about 12ft (4m) the choice is seemingly
boundless. Some very good traditional clinker-built
dinghies still exist; some of the family-orientated racing
classes are suitable for day sailing; then there are the
purpose-designed modern family dayboats which take
advantage of glassfibre construction to incorporate a
clever accommodation layout with plenty of stowage
space and built-in buoyancy.

A general purpose day sailing boat needs stability,
both inherent in the hull and directional stability under

way. That heart in the mouth, unsteady feeling
encountered on stepping gingerly aboard a racing
dinghy has no place here.

Stability and comfort are the prerequisites of a good
family dayboat. Lateral stability comes with full sections and a firm turn to the bilge, but the generous
waterline beam should not be carried all the way to the
transom. The after end of the hull should be tucked up
and narrowed a little to prevent the transom from
digging into the water. The weight of the helmsman
aggravates this tendency which, at best, creates drag
and slows the boat but at worst could drastically alter
the handling characteristics of the boat and perhaps
lead to a capsize.

A general purpose knockabout will have less rise of
floor – that is, a less sharply vee-d hull shape under the
water – than a thoroughbred. A racing dinghy,
however, may be considerably wider than her cruising
counterpart above the water: some racing boats which

do not carry trapeze or sliding seat have an exaggerated flare to minimize wetted area while providing the crew with the maximum practicable leverage to sit outboard and balance the rig.

A dinghy with narrow underwater sections will tend to instability and will not have the same comfortable carrying capacity as one with rounder underwater sections.

Comfort is not simply a question of taking a cushion afloat to sit on. Comfort is, to a large extent, the avoidance of discomfort – not being hit behind the ear by a large proportion of each passing wave, for example.

The bow of the boat is no place for over-full sections, neither should it be needle-sharp for its entire depth. The former will punch at the waves and make a lot of fuss for little forward progress, the latter will knife happily through the sea but, lacking reserve buoyancy will carry on knifing, maybe burying the bow under the next wave, building up a hobby-horse motion.

There should be a slight overhang forward (not too much, for speed is related to overall length at the waterline, not above it), a generous but not exaggerated flare in the topsides and a fine entry below the waterline. This boat will drive into the sea with the minimum of fuss and most of the spray will be deflected away from the crew by the flare of the hull itself. In dusty going some water is bound to find its way on to the foredeck; but washboards will stop most of the unwanted water infiltrating the cockpit.

A pram bow is often found in very small dinghies for the extra buoyancy, hence load-carrying ability, which it allows over a stem dinghy of similar length. It must be swept up so that the bow transom is well clear of the water when the boat is carrying her normal payload, and the weight of the crew and their gear should not be loaded too far forward or the bow will be depressed, the flat bow transom will slam into the waves and the boat will be stopped just as surely as a car which is driven into a bale of straw.

Gunwale rubbing strakes perform several useful functions besides acting as a buffer between a dinghy's topsides and anything she may hit or lie alongside. A generous rubbing strake will help to deflect spray and, ashore, will provide a handhold for lifting.

Buoyancy and stowage are often considered in the same breath, for often a buoyancy compartment will double as a stowage compartment when space is at a premium. Buoyancy here means reserve buoyancy, called upon to float a dinghy in the event of a capsize or immersion, so all compartments must be capable of being sealed effectively and easily. A block of foam or an inflated air bag should be carried in any buoyancy compartment which is not permanently sealed.

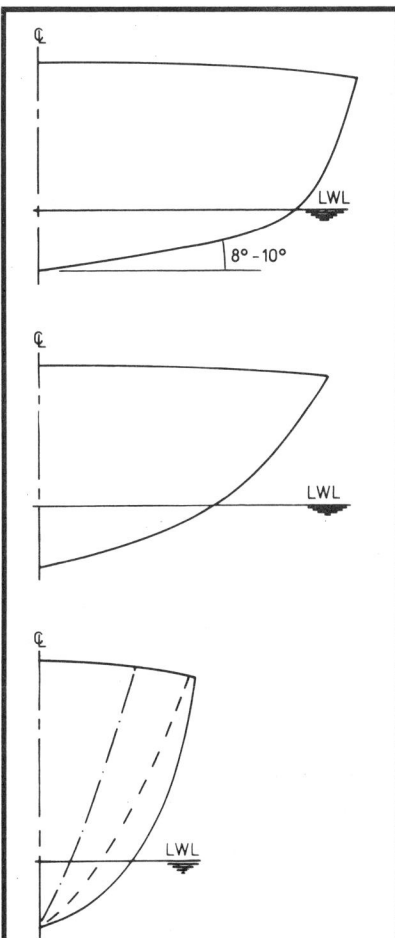

5.1a Dinghy hull sections (transverse). A stable hull shape suitable for general-purpose dinghies. A relatively wide waterline beam and firm turn of bilge contribute to stability; the flare above the water line helps to deflect spray and provides reserve buoyancey.
5.1b A much less stable section which might be found in some racing dinghies. The slack turn of bilge means that the boat will heel easily and could be difficult to control when heeled.
5.1c Bow sections. The outer shape is too full and will buffet into the waves and create much spray. The inner section, shown by the chain line, is rather fine and typical of some dinghies. The dotted line is about right for general-purpose boats.

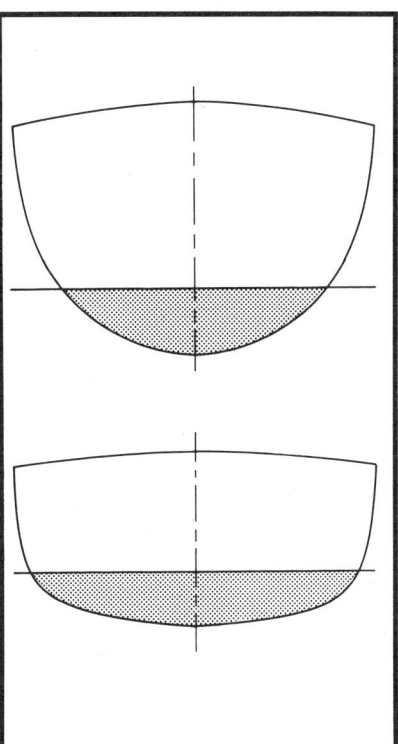

5.2 Designing is always a compromise. For a given displacement rounded sections (*top*) give less wetted surface than flat sections (*bottom*). But the rounded section shown has little inherent stability, while the flat section provides stability and is necessary for a planing hull.

The use of a bow transom on the little 10ft 10in (3.25m) Mirror results in a remarkably roomy dinghy for its size. *Martin Treadway*

And this is an International Fourteen, 70s style.

Distribution of buoyancy (or flotation) tanks is important. Reserve buoyancy in the floor alone is unsatisfactory, for when capsized the boat will tend to roll over completely and recovery will be difficult because the buoyant area must be pulled below the water before the boat can be righted. Too much reserve buoyancy is as bad as too little. Forward, aft and side tanks together can provide so much buoyancy that a capsized dinghy will float too high in the water to be manageable. Not only will it be impossible for a swimming crew to reach and climb on to the centreboard, but the boat will present so much area to the wind that she will blow away from the crew very fast indeed – possibly too fast even for a good swimmer to catch.

Ideally, there must be sufficient buoyancy to float the boat and her crew in safety while they bail. Dinghies which come upright with a lot of water aboard may suffer from water slopping up through the centreboard case as fast as the crew can bail. A daggerboard case must necessarily have an open top but a centreboard case can usually be at least partially closed by a capping piece.

Racing dinghies

It is not easy to spot where the cruising dinghy ends and the racing dinghy begins, particularly when one considers the well established dinghy classes. The earliest dinghy races were held in small open working boats and these developed into myriad similar, but subtly different, local designs, many of which were clinker built. Some of today's senior classes proudly trace their history back to the days of clinker building – classes like the International Fourteen, the class which introduced the planing hull to the sailing world in the shape of the Uffa Fox-designed 'Avenger' in 1928. In that year 'Avenger' won 52 of her 57 starts and was never out of the top three; she also sailed across the English Channel and back, three-up. It was the Fourteen, too, which introduced the trapeze: John Winter and Peter Scott sailed to victory in the class' Prince of Wales Cup race in 1937 using the device, but it was instantly banned from further competitions and it was not until 1969, many years after the worldwide acceptance of the trapeze, that the Fourteens relaxed their ban.

The Fourteen is an example of a restricted class – also known as a development class – whose development is allowed to progress within the bounds of rules which vary in their leniency from class to class. Two more extreme examples are the spectacularly over-canvassed 18ft (5.5m) Skiff (Sydney Harbour 18-footer) and the International Moth, 11ft (3.4m) of super-lightweight flier.

The traditional type of day racing keelboat: the crew stay where they belong – in the cockpit – relying on the weight of the keel to prevent the boat from heeling too far. *John Watney*

Anything you can do . . . A Hobie cat at play comes out to watch her big sisters a-racing.
John Watney

'I'll pull out the foot of the sail while you put some weight behind the main halyard'. The wind has dropped and it's time to shake out a reef. *John Watney*

A lot of sail, a lot of pulling power. But Canada's 'Dynamo' will need it all if she is to pull away from the blanketing effect of the huge rig of Argentina's 'Matrero' just astern. *John Watney*

A traditional turn of the century type of centreboarder. 18ft (5.5m) long and heavy enough to live on a mooring, this sort of dinghy is usually raced keenly in local events, fulfilling a secondary role as a picnicker. *Martin Treadway*

The one-design is limited by very tight specifications, from which it must not deviate at any point by more than the statutory few millimetres which are allowed for building tolerances.

Except in the case of boats like the Laser, Topper and Sunfish, all of which come from a single builder and some even from a single set of moulds, the pendulum within a one-design class will swing from one currently popular builder to another, from one momentarily fashionable sailmaker to another, with the same rapidity which may be expected of the development classes. A new sailmaker needs only one good regatta victory to fill his order books for months.

The performance of racing dinghies varies as much as the personalities of the people who race them. They can be quite sedate, with just one mainsail and jib; they can be fast planing boats with mainsail, genoa and vast spinnaker for off-the-wind work; or they can be single-handers, mostly una-rigged, of all shapes and sizes.

Unlike keelboats, dinghies are designed to be sailed on an even keel, and the weight of the crew is used to counter the pressure of the wind on the sail. In most classes the sail area is small enough to be controlled by the crew sitting on the sidedecks. As the wind increases, they hook their feet under toestraps and lean outboard so that their weight is as far removed as possible from the centreline. To exert the maximum righting moment some of the faster racing classes, which carry greater sail area, have an exaggerated flare in the topsides where the crew sit so that their weight can be sited a long way outboard in strong winds. Other classes allow the use of a trapeze or sliding seat (Chapter 3).

The racing dinghy tends to be leaner beneath the water than her general purpose sister; the knife-like bow and flat planing sections aft are typical of the more extreme racing classes. With very few exceptions, dinghies cannot sail sufficiently fast on a close-hauled course to lift and plane.

The most successful racing classes are not necessarily the fastest, most attractive or most spectacular. They tend to be the ones which best fit a variety of conditions and which have active owners' associations.

Good handicap racing like this is rare . . . *Martin Treadway*

Not everybody's cup of tea: the Bermuda Fitted Dinghy (it actually has a keep fin keel) presses on under a cloud of sail and really does need all those hands to turn corners. *Bermuda News Bureau*

. . . better to opt for a good regular turnout of a popular class at the local club for the best racing. *Martin Treadway*

The G.P. Fourteen, despite the adoption of a larger genoa some years back, retains its appeal as a husband and wife racing dinghy. G.P. stands for General Purpose: many keen owners have cruised extensively around local coasts and rivers. *Martin Treadway*

The fact that a dinghy does not carry a spinnaker does not necessarily make her uninteresting, but places a premium on teamwork between helmsman and crew. Those who make constant small adjustments will pull away from those who are content to cleat the sheets and break out the lemonade while waiting for the wind to do all the hard work. A boat with a spinnaker can even be an embarrassment – on small inland waters, for example, where conditions are fluky.

Joining the right class is easier than might be imagined from leafing through a dictionary of sailing boats. The temperament and physical condition of both skipper and crew are two of the most important factors: those who want to spend the maximum time afloat and the minimum time in the pits should avoid sensitive high-performance boats, for these tend to breed cut-throat racing demanding of much pre-race fiddling and tuning.

Some racing classes grew from general purpose designs which were marketed to meet the post-war sailing boom. A few owners would go to a regatta, form a class at the home club and, inevitably, seek improved performance. In some cases the racing modifications eventually precluded the lighter crews from competing in the class – the husband and wife teams for example – they would turn elsewhere and the whole cycle would start all over again.

Sailing venue should be considered carefully. Those relying on local competition with only the occasional foray to an open meeting will enjoy their racing more if they are part of a big fleet, not sailing the only boat of its type in a handicap fleet. The class which enjoys the best racing locally may not be an owner's first choice, but it will have proved itself suitable for local conditions, a point well worth remembering.

Those travelling the open meeting circuit need consider only the suitability of their physique, the ease of transportation of the boat on car roof or trailer and their compatibility with others already sailing in that class – their stable-mates for the season.

The loner will probably opt for a singlehander and here it really is vital to match physical type with the boat. There is a boat for every type: big and powerful for the heavy brigade; light and not too heavily canvassed for the lightweight; skitterish for the agile with a drip-dry outlook on life.

The Olympic Finn singlehander: underneath that rig is a big, heavy boat. Underneath that buoyancy jacket is a big, heavy skipper. *Les Cahiers du Yachting*

6 Keelboats

The word 'keelboat' has almost the same vagueness of meaning as the word 'boat' itself. Quite literally it means any boat with an external, fixed, ballasted keel – or two or even three keels as we shall see in the chapter on cruising boats.

The dayboat tends to be around 20ft (6m) in length, perhaps as small as 16ft, (5m) perhaps as large as 30ft (9m). Larger keelboats carry secondary classifications such as 'cruiser', 'cruiser-racer' or 'ocean racer', each of which we shall consider later, concerning these paragraphs only with day sailers, open racing boats and a few specialized larger racing keelboats of a certain type: a distinction which at first glance may be difficult to draw but which we hope will become apparent.

Cruising, so popular today, was hardly known at the turn of the century. Those who could afford to own a yacht naturally wished to prove the superiority of their boat over others and so almost all keelboats were built with racing in mind. At its initial peak of popularity, small keelboat racing (and here the word 'small' is used to distinguish the handier sizes up to 100ft (30m) or so from the mammoth schooners which preceded them) was dominated by measurement rules which encouraged long, slim yachts. Money was available to build boats which today we would regard as prohibitive, bearing in mind the singular use to which they were put. This breed did have accommodation below decks but it was not generally reckoned that an owner would actually wish to sleep on board; rather, that the paid hands would have somewhere to lay their heads during a short passage between one regatta venue and another.

Hence the daughters and grand-daughters of the type which survive today, the Metre Boats and their derivatives, are often considered as day racing boats, rather than cruiser/racers, despite their appreciable size. They can be, indeed often are, used for cruising but they tend to have an élitist appeal because of their proclivity to wetness, their limited accommodation for their length, and the amount of work which is needed to maintain them in tip-top condition. Very few have maintained sufficient momentum in new building to warrant the capital expense of glassfibre production.

Traditionally, an owner commissioning a new yacht would approach a designer who would supply him with a unique design. Each yacht would be a one-off and this philosophy automatically extended to the early racing boats. They would race to handicaps worked out by the race committee but as rating rules (rules governing measurement, or rating) were introduced, boats of a certain rating would race together, on level terms.

It was not until the early years of the twentieth century that the sailing world fully appreciated the advantages of the one-design: that is, a whole fleet of boats built to a single set of lines. Financially, such a concept was advantageous because only a single designer's fee was required to be paid, with a relatively small royalty on each subsequent boat built. The builder, too, could effect some economies with the knowledge that he would be building other similar boats. Racing became closer, placing a premium on the helmsman's expertise and the boat handling ability of his crew, rather than on the depth of the owner's pocket.

Today, racing keelboat classes rejoice in fancy names, like Tempest and Dragon. Romance until the mid-twentieth century was to be found in the graceful lines of the boats themselves or in the owner's choice of individual name, for the classes were known merely by their rating level – 23 Metre, J Class and so on.

The early and larger Metre Boats still raced on handicap. A boat would be given a time allowance and her corrected time would be calculated at the end of the race by applying her time allowance to her elapsed time. As designers took advantage of the rules, a greater degree of conformity was apparent in boats built to a specific rating and these began to race on equal terms, with no time allowances.

5.5 Metres. *Australian Information Service*

The Metre Boat classes which survive today are relatively few, for it is a costly business to build a sizeable one-off for the often limited racing which is available. Most prestigious may be said to be the Twelve Metre and it is to this class that many leading designers devote much research and development. But in truth the breed is being kept alive as a racing class only for its involvement with the classic America's Cup match race (of which more in Chapter 13).

The Twelve, as she is raced today, makes no pretence at accommodation but the smaller 30 sq Metres (sail area is restricted to 30 sq m), Eight Metres and Six Metres often fulfil a dual role as cruiser/racers. This type of boat has found favour particularly on large areas of sheltered water where light winds prevail: there are, for example, many modern one-designs which reflect Metre Boat thinking on the Swiss Lakes.

Smallest of the true Metre Boat classes is the Five

The long, lean, almost Metre Boat type of hull is still very popular on big lakes with flat water. This one is an instruction boat of the Lake Thun (Switzerland) Sailing School.

point Five Metre which ousted the Six Metre in the yachting section of the Olympic Games soon after the second world war and was itself ousted, principally on financial grounds by the one-design Dragon. But the much-loved Dragon was another elderly design and the International Yacht Racing Union organized a design competition and set of trials for a new three-man keelboat suitable for Olympic competition.

Such trials have a history of acrimony, procrastination and at the end of the day a tendency to produce the wrong result. The Contender singlehander and the Australis catamaran were both the products of such trials and neither has yet gained any appreciable international popularity nor shown any sign of being adopted for Olympic competition. However the Soling, winner of the keelboat trials from a very worthy field, turned out to be a truly popular boat in its own right and a most attractive one, though totally different from the Dragon whose Olympic status she was to usurp in 1972. She confirmed the trend in modern day-racing keelboats towards less fixed ballast in the fin itself but

The Dragon, which ousted the 5.5 Metre from Olympic competition . . . *Studio 77*

. . . and was in its turn ousted by the Soling. This photograph was taken in the early days, when chest harnesses were not allowed, and sitting out like this for hours on end called for iron muscles. *Studio 77*

The dinghy-like performance of that most dinghy-like of keelboats, the Tempest. *Ian Proctor*

more hung over the windward side in the shape of members of the crew. For several years Soling crews slumped right out over the edge with only toestraps to support them, only their heels in contact with the horizontal surface of the sidedeck. In later years, they have been allowed to wear chest harnesses and hook themselves to support lines attached to the boat, to relieve the strain on their backs.

Perhaps the most extreme modern racing keelboat, and one which can fairly be said to be a cross between a dinghy and a keelboat, is the two-man Tempest which enjoyed Olympic status for just two Olympiads. The Tempest has a dinghy-like hull with self-draining cockpit, a lifting keel with ballasted bulb (though owners rarely take advantage of the lifting facility) and a trapeze for the crew. Because she has so little ballast in her keel, the Tempest calls for a big, tough crew and belies the belief that keelboats are uncapsizeable. Many a Tempest has been knocked flat in a strong wind, but a flattened Tempest is nonetheless a smaller problem than a capsized dinghy because her keel will help her upright again when the gust passes.

A far cry from the Tempest is the boat which she displaced from the Olympics – and which, curiously, replaced her in turn: the Star. Designed in 1911, the boxy Star carries an enormous spread of sail, mostly in the mainsail, and for most of her racing life was not allowed toestraps. This led to the crew lying prone along the windward gunwale to keep his weight as far to windward as possible, hence the description 'hiking Star-boat fashion'.

Not every keelboat sailor interests himself in the Olympics, of course, and there are many, many keelboat classes: certainly as many as there are dinghy classes, although they are necessarily more thinly spread throughout the world because of the greater financial outlay required for the larger boat, and because their owners travel less frequently, if at all, to regattas away from home. Much keelboat sailing is carried on at local level, the boat being lifted out of the water only once a year for an annual overhaul.

Many racing keelboats are suited also for family picnics and day sailing, in fact there are very few day-sailers which have been expressly designed for the role. The less extreme racing machines offer the comfort and stability required of the day sailer; the ability to lay at a mooring until required and to be handled easily by any member of the family who finds a spare moment for a singlehanded spin.

Then there is the oldie, the local one-design which developed from the local working boat and which now is cherished by a handful of owners almost as a family pet, handed down through the generations and brought out in all her glory to race on high days, holidays and

A squib and a Flying Fifteen, both about 20ft (6m) overall and both popular for racing and for day-sailing. *Studio 77*

The extra effort of transporting and launching a keelboat over that required for a dinghy restrict owners' participation in 'away games'. *Wendy Fitzpatrick*

The Royal Anglesey Fife class, at 26ft (8m) is still raced keenly on
its home waters of the Menai Straits. *William G. Rowntree*

Another local Menai Straits class, the 20ft (6m) Hilbre Island One Design, has a vestigial keel which houses a lifting centreboard and a day cuddy for protection against the worst of the elements. *William G. Rowntree*

regatta days. It is invidious to try to draw a distinction here between the centreboarder and the keelboat. There may be only a couple of inches of difference in the overall length and very little in the overall weight or in the lines. Since we are talking here of boats over about 16ft (4.8m) in length, it can be assumed that centreboarder and keelboat alike will live on a mooring during the sailing season.

. . . fflying along!

7 Suitable clothing

Sailing clothing, though it may look like a rather indifferent form of fancy dress to the non-sailing man, has been developed to fulfil a specific function.

There is a type of apparel for every branch of the sport. It is no use, for example, going afloat in a slow, rather wet cruising boat wearing the type of wetsuit beloved of dinghy sailors and expecting to stay warm. Conversely, a full suit of oilskins will render the wearer quite useless in a busy dinghy race.

It *is* possible to combine fashion with practicality . . . but only just. The dedicated follower of fashion has a wealth of trendy p.v.c. clothing to choose from, the minority of which will keep its wearer dry in really rough weather. So, before buying a garment for its looks, it is wise to seek the candid advice of an unbiased third party on its suitability for the task it will have to perform. If the wearer merely wants a splash-proof garment, all well and good; if he or she will have to stand his or her watch on deck in the middle of a stormy night, he or she will begin to care less about appearances than about weatherproofness.

Dinghies

Fair-weather pottering calls for little more than jeans or shorts, non-slip canvas shoes, a lightweight anorak and a buoyancy aid plus however many sweaters the temperature dictates.

Dinghy racing is an entirely different kettle of fish. The crew must be warm and comfortable throughout the race, which may be held in a frizzling light weather drifter or in a fearsome winter gale. Surprisingly, a single wetsuit will fill the bill in most weathers.

A one-piece style is the most comfortable, eliminating as it does the discomfort of the double midriff layer and the possibility that the overlap twixt jacket and trousers will gape at the strategic moment and let in a douche of cold water. In hot climates a sleeveless shortie will be sufficient, in temperate and cooler areas a sleeveless long-john is ideal, allowing the wearer to adjust the number of sweaters he wears for the conditions prevailing on the day.

Early sailing wetsuits, developed from those used by skin divers, were stiff and cumbersome and although modern Neoprene has largely eliminated any stiffness, there remains the tendency in all but the most expensively-designed styles to restrict circulation at joints which must bend and move – the knees, shoulders and elbows. By opting for a sleeveless style, two of these constricting areas are removed, leaving only the knees which move less frequently and less energetically.

A long-john on its own will be sufficient protection for warmer days; with a thin polo neck sweater underneath and any number of thicker sweaters over the top, it can be topped by an anorak or a one-piece proofed nylon oversuit in cool winds. A long-john with matching bolero is a useful combination for winter sailing.

The whole purpose of a wetsuit is to trap a layer of water and air next to the skin and to keep it warm. Used dry, it can be surprisingly cold; used wet on an inactive body, it can be colder still, which is why it is of little use to the passenger of a small open motorboat or keelboat.

Keelboats

Once out of the realms of dinghy-like activities – and here we include those serious racing keelboats whose crews spend a great deal of active time being soaked by spray – wetsuits are no longer *de rigeur*.

The traditional wear of the keelboat crew is casual slacks or jeans, shirt and sweater(s) topped by oilskins and a towel around the neck when the weather dictates.

Oilies need no longer be the heavy, traditional oilskin fabric: supple cotton- or nylon-backed p.v.c. and proofed nylon fabrics have proved themselves to be excellent at keeping the water where it belongs while allowing a previously unknown freedom of move-

Fair-weather pottering: shorts, shirts, buoyancy aid . . . remember sun-tan cream, sweater, anorak in case the weather changes.

Ready for sea: heavy duty proofed nylon ocean-racer suit with integral buoyancy lung and safety harness.

ment . . . but they do rely on the skill of the designer and manufacturer.

A cheap 'waterproof' suit is a false economy. It must have seams which are welded, not merely stitched, or the water will penetrate the stitch holes. It must have double storm fastenings and snug-fitting, watertight wrists and necks which do not chafe.

Chest-high trousers are more comfortable than those with a simple elasticated waist. If choosing a heavy proofed-nylon fabric for the suit, it is worth investing a little extra in lined, rather than unlined garments to reduce the risk of condensation.

Hoods can be a nuisance; very few turn with the wearer's head and an old fashioned sou'wester takes a lot of beating.

Under-garments made of synthetic pile fabric are used universally by serious crews for their warmth, lightness and ease of washing and drying. These so-called Polar Suits were developed for climbers and polar adventurers and it didn't take the sailing world long to appreciate their value.

Extremities

Gloves are essential on modern racing boats, to save the wearer's hands from the thin lines which are used increasingly in the interests of weight saving aboard. Essential, too, for winter sailing, to offer some protection and to save cold hands from excess chafe. Most sailing gloves are made of a type of chromed leather which, though it may dry hard, is very supple when wet. Palms will be reinforced and elasticated gussets will be provided in the fingers. The fingers and thumbs will probably have open ends to allow the wearer to perform the more fiddly jobs on board.

Sunhats and glasses can be of use in hot weather, but only if they stay in place without constant adjustment. A film producer-type sun peak can be of great value to a spinnaker hand and suntan lotion or barrier cream is essential on all bare skin exposed to the sun afloat.

Footwear varies according to the season and the type of boat. Blue canvas deck shoes are being superseded by hide styles in many colours. Neoprene wetsuit socks are widely used in dinghies, special ankle-length dinghy boots are available, reinforced for sitting out and trapezing; offshore crews tend to use knee-length boots . . .but all have one thing in common: good non-slip rubber soles.

Sailing clothing is not just a cult – neither does it bear much resemblance to the fashion photographer's idea of what the nattily dressed yachtsman is wearing this year, my dear. Like the horseman or horsewoman's jodphurs, its function is comfort with neatness with practicality.

8 Rules of the road at sea

You can't just buy a boat and sail it hither and thither without falling foul of the rulemaker. Some countries have more rules than others governing the registration of boats and the equipment they must carry – indeed such rules vary between different water and·harbour authorities in a single country – so we shall restrict this resumé to the two truly international sets of regulations which apply to sailing folk.

International Regulations for Preventing Collisions at Sea

When steamships first plied the same waters as the great sailing ships a regulation came into being which required power to give way to sail. This is arguably the most often misquoted and misused regulation among the uninformed sailing fraternity. It is quite true that the pleasure power cruiser is required to manoeuvre to keep clear of sailing craft; it is not true that the skipper of a sailing boat can charge full tilt at, say, a coaster or a fishing boat and demand right of way.

The International Regulations are framed with manoeuvrability in mind, rather than the method of propulsion. It is simply not feasible for a supertanker, with the reaction time of a dinosaur, to manoeuvre to keep clear of a smaller vessel unless its captain receives due notice several miles (kilometres) away. Even then, that tanker may be threading its way along a narrow dredged channel with only a few feet (a metre or so) of water under its immense keel.

It is not practicable for a fishing boat, with nets cast, to transport itself suddenly to another area just to save the crew of a sailing boat putting in an extra·tack.

It is potentially dangerous, certainly expensive, to try to force a commercial ship out of the main channel in a river or estuary. The average yacht's third party liability insurance cover begins to look inadequate with each successive tide which fails to refloat the cargo ship which went aground while avoiding her.

And so the Regulations are framed to allow unwieldy craft right of way both in restricted waters and over more manoeuvrable vessels. For all practical purposes, sailing boats come quite high on the priority list, powerboats (however oblivious their owners may sometimes appear to be of their obligations) come right at the bottom.

These are the main points and they apply to everything which crosses the water, including amphibious cars, seaplanes, hovercraft and hydrofoils:–

○ Every vessel is required to maintain a proper lookout. This includes an occasional peep under the foot of the genoa and means that, however bad the conditions, someone must regularly turn into the wind and spray to see whether there is a situation building up to windward

○ Taking into account the visibility, traffic density, weather conditions and manoeuvrability of the vessel, a safe speed must be maintained.

○ Every effort must be made to avoid the risk of collision. It is easy to determine whether two boats are on a collision course by taking regular compass bearings on the second boat as she approaches. If a constant bearing is maintained, Someone has to Do Something. If the other boat alters course, it is just possible that her bearing will not change so a check must be maintained until it is obvious that the two courses are diverging.

○ Action to avoid a collision must be taken in good time and should be a good, clear change of course in the correct direction so that the skipper of the other boat is left in no doubt that he may proceed in safety.

○ In a restricted channel, drive on the right – or, to put it in more nautical terms, keep as far as possible to the starboard side of the fairway.

. . . as can driving spray to windward. *Roger M. Smith*

There could be a lot of wind under these clouds and that will mean a lot of hard work and acrobatics for the competitors in this OK dinghy championship. *Wendy Fitzpatrick*

Drying out. *Wendy Fitzpatrick*

A view that far too many enjoyed of the high-scoring German 'Pinta' and the Irish 'Irish Mist II'
in the 1975 Admiral's Cup series. *John Watney*

In a glassfibre-dominated age, a lovely wooden boat is a sight for sore eyes. *John Watney*

A deck-sweeping genoa can seriously impair vision to leeward . . .
Ajax News Photos

○ When two sailing boats meet, the one with the wind on her port side – that is, the one on port tack or gybe – gives way to the other. If they are both on the same tack the one to leeward keeps clear.

○ An overtaking boat has no right of way over the boat she is passing.

○ When two powerboats are destined for a head-on collision they should each alter course to starboard. Funny how this simple requirement seems to confuse so many skippers in the heat of the moment.

Lights, shapes and sounds

The multiplicity of signals shown and made by the various categories of seagoing craft is outside the scope of this book. Suffice it to say that the boat owner venturing away from the safety of the shore should be armed with an up to date copy of the Regulations and a colour chart of signals.

'Every effort must be made to avoid the risk of collision'. *Jonathan Eastland*

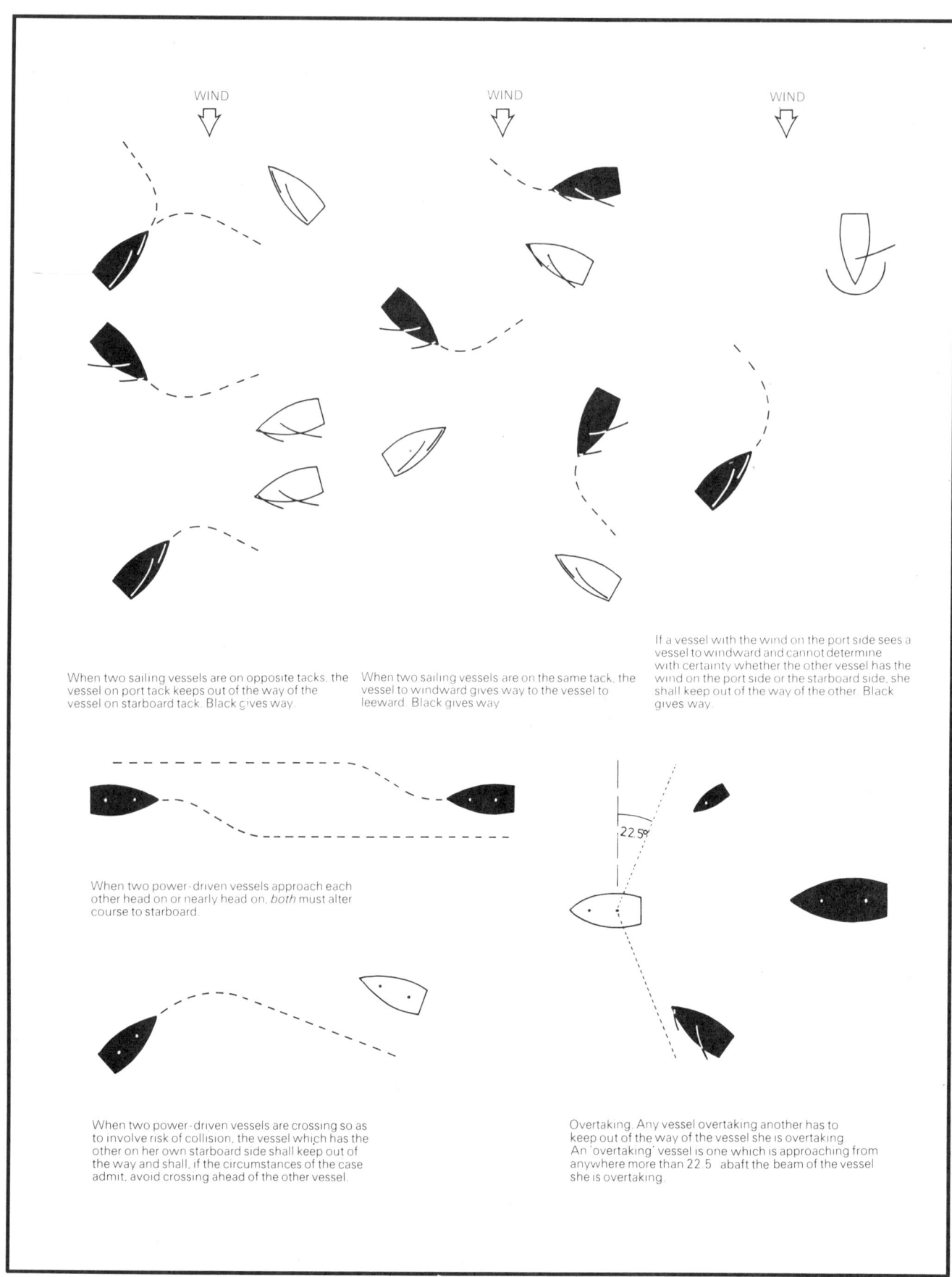

WIND

WIND

WIND

When two sailing vessels are on opposite tacks, the vessel on port tack keeps out of the way of the vessel on starboard tack. Black gives way.

When two sailing vessels are on the same tack, the vessel to windward gives way to the vessel to leeward. Black gives way.

If a vessel with the wind on the port side sees a vessel to windward and cannot determine with certainty whether the other vessel has the wind on the port side or the starboard side, she shall keep out of the way of the other. Black gives way.

When two power-driven vessels approach each other head on or nearly head on, *both* must alter course to starboard.

22.5°

When two power-driven vessels are crossing so as to involve risk of collision, the vessel which has the other on her own starboard side shall keep out of the way and shall, if the circumstances of the case admit, avoid crossing ahead of the other vessel.

Overtaking. Any vessel overtaking another has to keep out of the way of the vessel she is overtaking. An 'overtaking' vessel is one which is approaching from anywhere more than 22.5 abaft the beam of the vessel she is overtaking.

Youngsters learning their racing technique in small boats like these Mirrors soon get to grips with the right of way rules. *Martin Treadway*

Small sailing yachts are required to show only red (port) and green (starboard) sidelights and a white sternlight at night and these may be combined in a single masthead light. It is prudent to carry the required lights as high as possible for the deck of a small sailing boat is frequently lost to sight in the trough of a wave. If she is under power she must carry a white steaming light on her mast, shining forward.

Power driven vessels, depending on overall length, show one or two white masthead lights, sidelights and a sternlight when under way. Anchored craft, fishing boats, trawlers, tugs, dredgers and those manoeuvring in restricted waters all have different light signals to convey their actions. By day, lights are replaced by shapes – two black balls, for example, indicate a vessel not under command; three indicate a vessel aground.

Sound signals can vary from port to port but the principal ones which will convey to the sailing man the intentions of the steamer he thought he would cross in safety are:–

○ one short blast means 'I am altering my course to starboard'.

○ two short blasts mean 'I am altering my course to port'.

○ three short blasts mean 'I am going astern'.

Racing Rules

Despite what the pundits say, it is not necessary to be able to quote chapter and verse on every innuendo of every racing rule at every mark of the course. Those who can, will amuse themselves for hours discussing the finer points of a situation; those who cannot may well have avoided that situation and picked up a few positions into the bargain.

Every sport must have its rules and most have an umpire, or referee, to see that the rules are observed. While this may be possible in theory at the turning

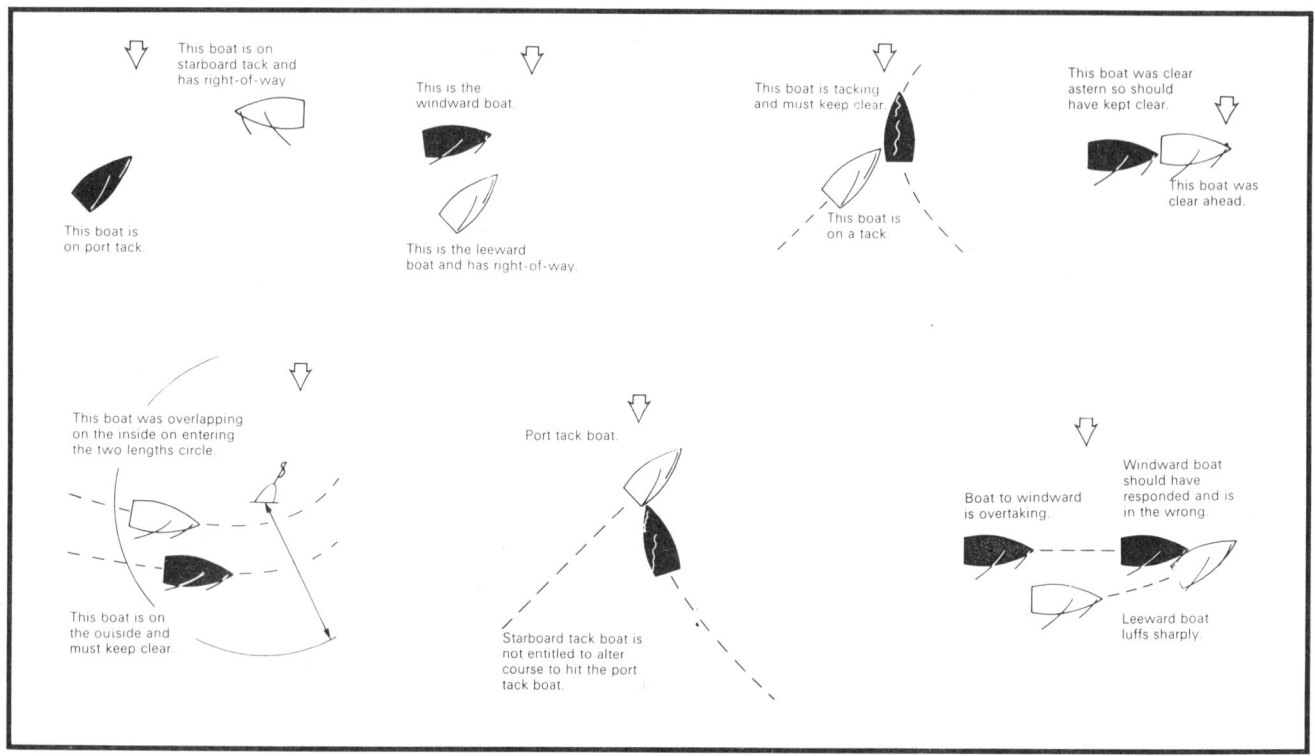

The most thorough knowledge of the racing rules won't prevent an occasional misjudgment: this dinghy skipper has gone for the start too early and become entangled with others waiting for the gun. *Frank Chapman*

marks of a short course, in practice a whole army of umpires could never hope to monitor every movement in a yacht race. So it is left to the competitors themselves to play fair – and to lodge a protest against a misdemeaning fellow competitor when the need arises. Some clubs go as far as to require the helmsman of a boat to sign a declaration after finishing a race that he has abided by all the rules.

When a protest is lodged a mini-court room drama takes place with the two combatants and their respective witnesses being cross-examined by members of the protest committee, who decide who was right or wrong on the evidence presented and disqualify the miscreant from the race, assuming he can be identified as such.

In recent years the adoption of alternative penalties for those who admit they have broken a rule has received widespread approval. Instead of being forced to retire from the race – perhaps for an inconsequential error like touching a mark of the course while rounding it – the victim may now sail round in circles twice (known as performing a 720° turn) or accept a percentage penalty, depending on the conditions of the race. It is usually the offshore racing yachts which adopt the time penalty system, the percentage simply being added to their corrected time, while the more manoeuvrable dinghies are free to perform their gyrations and catch up again if they are fast enough.

Some of the racing rules lean heavily on the International Regulations for Preventing Collisions at

'. . . without falling foul of the rulemaker' *Robert O'Neill*

Sea. A port tack boat, for example, must give way to a starboard tack boat; a windward boat must keep clear of the boat to leeward and an overtaking boat must keep clear of the boat she is overtaking.

Other important rules to be remembered are:–

○ that a boat which is tacking or gybing must keep clear of a boat which is not.

○ a boat which is clear astern of another must keep clear.

○ a boat which is overlapped by another at a turning mark or obstruction must give the inside boat room to round.

○ a right of way boat must not alter course in a way which would prevent others from keeping clear. Sim-

ilarly she must not manoeuvre into a right of way position so close to another boat that the other has no chance of avoiding a collision.

The only time when a boat is allowed to make a sharp alteration of course in order to defend her position is when another is challenging her to windward. In this case she is within her rights to luff into the wind (but not beyond head to wind) to baulk the other's progress but she must curtail that luff the moment the helmsman of the other boat, in his normal position, is in line with the luffing boat's mast.

Each important manoeuvre is defined by the International Yacht Racing Union, the administering body which is responsible for the rules. A tack, for example, does not start when the helmsman starts to push the tiller to leeward, but at the moment the bow of the boat passes through the eye of the wind. A tack is

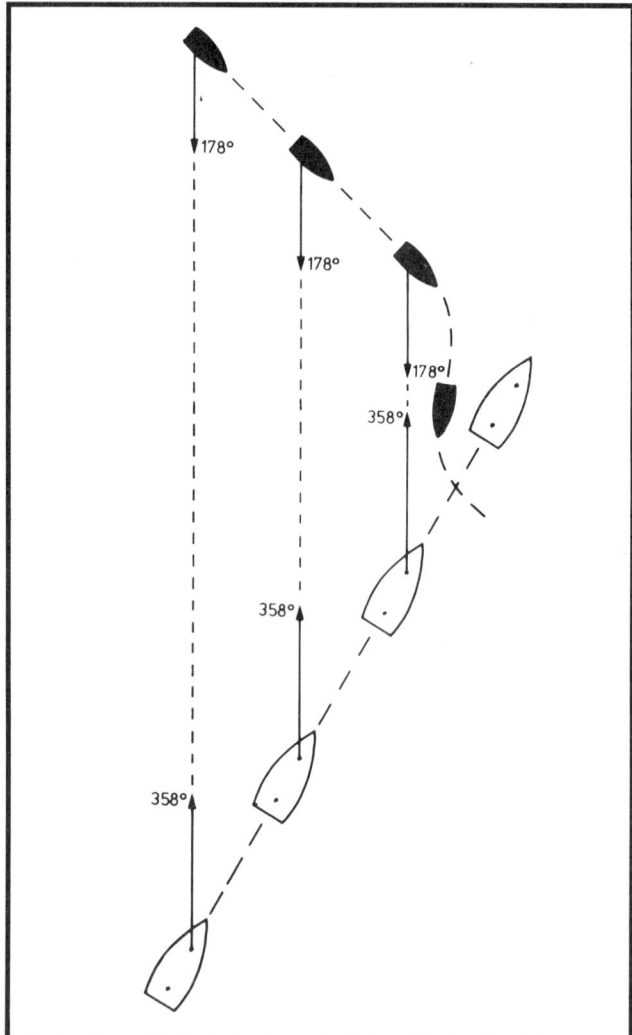

178°

178°

178°

178°

358°

358°

358°

358°

8.3 Converging courses. If the true bearing of another vessel remains the same, both vessels are on a collision course. The giving-way vessel must alter course.

completed when the boat's sails are full on the new tack. An overlap at a mark must be established at a distance from the mark equal to two overall lengths of the longer boat.

Mark rounding is fraught with potential rule situations – made more complicated for the novice by the apparent anomaly that the rule he is taught is sacrosanct, namely that port tack gives way to starboard, is actually over-ridden on occasion at a mark. Approaching a windward mark, a port tack boat must give way to a starboard tack boat, whether or not the starboard tacker reckons she has an overlap. On a downwind leg, however, a starboard tacker may have to allow a port tacker room to round the mark if she has established a correct overlap.

All this points to the advisability of studying the rule book before indulging in close tactical sailing. And not just the rules which govern the relative positions of boats during the course of a race: there are some very important prohibitions under a section entitled 'Obligations of Helmsman and Crew in Handling a Yacht'. The requirement, for example, to set only one spinnaker boom and to ensure that it is always carried on the opposite side of the boat from the main boom; the description of a correct course, which urges the helmsman to consider his wake as a piece of string which, when drawn tight, would pass each mark of the course on the correct side; the rights of a boat which is anchored, aground or capsized and the limitations which are placed on the flapping of sails, waggling of rudders, dramatic alteration of trim and rocking of hulls which are known under the collective descriptive heading of pumping, ooching and rocking.

Oh no, competitive sailboat racing is not just a matter of sailing round the course.

9 Cruisers

Let it not be suggested that there is a single, stereotype, form of cruising boat. For cruising is arguably the branch of sailing which attracts the widest disparity of personalities, from the sybarite to the masochist. Their own psyche is reflected in their choice of boat.

Neither is there a single type of sailing involved. Cruising at its most basic can be undertaken in a 12ft (3.6m) dinghy equipped with an air bed, camping stove, bucket and cockpit cover: it is a game for the hardy, but these hardies are by no means impecunious youngsters. Take the case of Frank Dye who has cruised both singlehanded and accompanied by his wife, Margaret, in a 16ft (4.8m) Wayfarer as far from his native English shores as Norway. But this level of involvement is to be recommended only to the very experienced specialist – and then only with reservations.

The smallest true cruiser need be little more than a dinghy with a lid; the largest, one of those dreamships which ply fashionable Bahamian marinas with charter parties of bronzed jet-setters. To fulfil their various roles, all must boast a high degree of seaworthiness, comfort and handiness in relation to their size and be well equipped for the task they are asked to perform.

The hull must take the waves in her stride, neither slamming nor knifing through to soak the entire crew, wherever they may be stationed, and the boat must not heel dramatically to the slightest gust of wind.

The beamier a boat, the greater the inherent stability of her hull – a fact which can readily be appreciated by folding a sheet of cardboard into a narrow V shape and comparing its stability against that of a square box on the nearest village pond. However, the V shape will travel more easily through the water than the square box given the same amount of propulsion. The tendency of the V shape to heel over can be inhibited by the addition of a ballasted keel, but this adds weight and is in itself a slowing factor. So the designer must decide on a happy medium to suit the purpose of the

Some tiny cruisers are no more than dinghies with lids . . . but they are ideal for exploring sheltered creeks and rivers. *Martin Treadway*

boat and the extent to which her crew will be working her; whether they will be constantly driving her hard, as in a racing boat, or whether they wish the boat to look after herself while they sit back and enjoy just being afloat, which is the purpose of a cruising boat.

Now return to the metaphorical village pond and take a second V shape card hull, attaching it parallel to the first. This twin-hull configuration still offers less resistance to forward movement than the box shape but

Time to think about taking in a reef or lowering the spinnaker . . .
or both. Notice how the helmsman is having to hold the tiller well
up to windward to prevent the boat from turning up into the
wind. *Studio 77*

does not need the extra weight of a ballasted keel to
keep it upright. This is the advantage of the catamaran:
needing less weight she can be constructed more lightly
than a heavy keelboat yet she has ample inherent
stability to enable her to carry a good spread of sail for
speed. But there is no built-in heart-in-the-mouth safety
factor with a cat: when a keelboat heels, the crew know
at a certain angle that it is time to shorten sail. A cat
heels – or flies a hull – quite suddenly and if a really
vicious gust hits just as she is approaching this point she
may capsize. She is as stable upside-down as she is the
right way up and rescue becomes necessary.

A racing boat can be cruised, but in her raw state
usually not with any degree of comfort and usually not
by a short-handed crew. Over the years measurement
rules have encouraged certain features in boats which
are built to race under them, features which individually can be of benefit to the cruising man but
which collectively point to racing speed rather than
cruising comfort. The long, or full, keel of the 50s is a
good underwater configuration for a cruising boat
which spends most of her time in deep water. The
latterday narrow fin keel and separate skeg-hung
rudder is not, for the very responsiveness it bestows
upon the racing boat is the opposite of the cruising
man's needs. He needs a boat which will continue on
course, perfectly balanced, while he leaves the helm to
effect a sail change or brew a cup of coffee. The right rig

allied to a long keel will give him this facility, whereas a boat with separate fin keel and rudder profile will tend to be skitterish, lacking in directional stability and demanding of constant attention to the wheel or tiller.

The modern racing boat does have one bonus over her predecessors in the matter of cruising suitability, and that is a voluminous hull into which may be packed a previously unheard of degree of accommodation. So the good modern cruising boat can look just like her racing sisters, taking advantage of traditional sea-worthy features with the opportunity to provide luxurious living below.

At the other end of the scale is the traditional workboat conversion. Of robust construction, she probably displays a pleasing chunkiness under a gaff rig. Her value has been proved as a seaboat, generations of fishermen, perhaps, having worked her in all weathers with only the minimum of crew. Builders of many motor-sailers (or fifty-fifties as they are sometimes known) and so-called character craft often draw their inspiration from the lines of the workboat – and who's to decry the principle? It maintains a semblance of traditionalism, even if those tanned sails reveal themselves, upon closer inspection, to be made of modern synthetic sailcloth and if the sound of modern ball-bearing winches has replaced the creak of the wooden sheave block.

Keels

We have touched briefly on the underwater appendages of the cruising boat, but the fin keel is by no means the only method of providing ballast. In fact, it can be a positive embarrassment – in shoal waters, for example, where there is the constant risk of grounding, or on a drying mooring or anchorage.

The twin-keel configuration has found wide acceptance for estuary cruising. External ballast is carried in two fairly shallow keels attached to the hull on either side of the centreline – towards the turn of the bilge, hence her other description of bilge-keeler. These enable the boat to sit upright when she takes the ground and render life on board appreciably more comfortable than if the boat dries out at an acute angle of heel. Twin keels do have an adverse effect on the boat's sailing performance, however, particularly on the wind. Lacking the deep bite of the single keel, she will make more leeway than the fin-keel boat and it is the rare and extreme cases of clumsily-designed, under-canvassed, badly-prepared twin-keeled boats coming to grief on a lee shore which encourage the supporters of the fin keel to heap derision upon the breed.

The twin keels' greatest advantage can also be their greatest disadvantage. Such a boat is designed to sit

Careful interior planning ensures that the case for the lifting keel on this 20-footer (6m) is an integral part of the accommodation, rather than an eyesore. The T-shape cut-outs on the galley bulkhead are for stowage of plates and cups, which are 'posted' through the upper slot and remain in place at sea.

upright when she takes the ground. However, if she accidentally touches bottom while sailing it may be impossible to persuade her to claw off again before the tide drops, unless she first hit when heeled. If a fin keel boat goes aground, it is frequently possible to sail or motor her off quickly by heeling her an exaggerated amount, thus reducing her draught. Heeling a twin keel boat serves only to increase that draught, hence reduce the possibility of making a clean getaway.

Three keels are also common. The main, centre keel will be a full keel carrying most of the ballast and the two bilge keels will in effect be legs, to support the boat aground in an upright position.

Lifting keels and centreboards are becoming increasingly popular, as builders are devoting more expertise to interior design. The box which houses the keel need no longer be an eyesore and an impediment to accommodation: it can be utilized in the cabin layout so that it is barely noticeable.

Rig

The best cruising rig is one which offers variety. It is essential that each sail may be handled easily by one

Drying out: but with a triple keel configuration, the boat will
remain more or less upright until the tide returns. *J.S. Biscoe*

crew member, with perhaps just the occasional helping hand from a second. It is easy to appreciate, then, that huge spinnakers and masthead genoas have no place in the everyday sail wardrobe of the average cruising boat. Floaters (large, lightweight spinnakers) and ghosters (large, lightweight headsails) are useful luxuries in very light weather but their omission is no cause for concern.

It is this necessity to keep the manageability of each sail within the realms of one man which endears the gaff rig to so many cruising yachtsmen.

The sloop rig is, however, a more simple rig, hence a cheaper rig for the builder of a production boat to supply to his customers. Those family cruisers whose rig emulates the masthead rig of the modern racing boat may look very flash but will be less handy over a range of conditions than those which set a more balanced rig, with a moderate size mainsail and headsail, rather than a tiny mainsail and over-large genoa. The masthead genoa of the offshore racer is excellent for windward work but rather an embarrassment downwind, as is the tiny mainsail, for it is the mainsail which is truly the main sail of the cruising boat and called on to keep the boat driving on all points of sailing.

Given efficient reefing gear, a cruiser can make do with a single mainsail. Her wardrobe of headsails should include a stormsail, small in area and well made of heavy cloth, a working jib for brisk to strong winds and a No. 1 jib for medium breezes.

A cutter rig can be carried to good effect for cruising and above 30ft (10m) or so a ketch or yawl rig becomes a workable proposition. The use of a schooner rig on boats of less than about 45ft (13.5m) is something of a gimmick.

Equipment

In considering accommodation, deck layout and equipment it is necessary first to consider the role a boat is required to fill. Even Lloyd's Register of Shipping, the society which lays down the minimum scantlings and equipment for boats constructed to the famous 100A1 classification, has a special niche for boats which are to be used solely on sheltered inland waters. Such a boat, required for only short day trips and estuary pottering, may justifiably dispense with some of the items which are so vital for extended passage making.

Ground Tackle

A good basic wardrobe of sails is necessary if a boat is to sail efficiently in all *reasonable* weathers. Good ground tackle is even more essential, for this will be called upon to assist her to remain on station in *all* weathers. The lightweight grapple, descriptively known as a lunch-

Moderation is the key to a good cruising rig: each sail should be easily handled by one man. *Press Photos International*

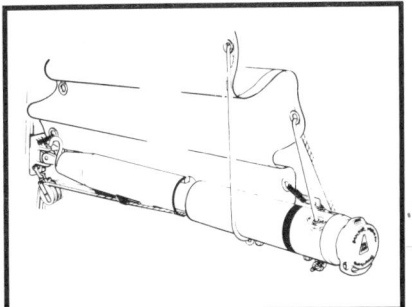

9.1 Slab reefing. The luff cringle is slipped over the hook near the gooseneck. The slab line aft, which hauls down the first reef cringle, is led internally through the boom.

Taking in a reef in good time. Notice the reinforcing patches around the reefing eyes in the sail.

The popular cutter rig; 'White Mouse' was built in 1870 of timber left over from a Brixham Trawler. *Martin Treadway*

hook, tied to the end of a length of light line is fine for the short picnic stop but totally inadequate as the sole means of anchoring.

A good, heavy anchor should always be ready for use and it should be used with chain, not rope. If chain is used it is the weight of the anchor cable itself which holds the boat, the anchor serving to locate the chain in the required position on the sea bed. It is folly to save weight in the ground tackle because it is that weight which will hold the boat: the chain must be heavy enough – and long enough – to hold the boat in a tidal stream.

If a rope cable, or even part-rope cable is used the pull of the boat is transferred to the anchor which may well be pulled free if the holding ground is not very good. There is the additional risk that rope will become tangled round the boat's keel as she swings to the turn of the tide.

Stowage

A heavy, wet, muddy anchor is an unsociable item and must be provided with secure stowage, out of the way of

those working on deck yet ready for instant use. The ideal stowage is a drained, covered well recessed into the foredeck at the bow with the chain disappearing down a chainpipe into a drained chain locker. Where such stowage is impracticable on smaller boats the anchor must be secured in stout chocks on the foredeck and the chain must never, never be allowed to lay loose.

Stowage for fenders, spare lines, oars, buckets, outboard engine, fishing tackle and all the other 'outdoor' paraphernalia should ideally be provided in cockpit lockers. Lockers, note. Several medium size lockers are better than one cavernous maw which swallows every item it is fed and automatically re-stows it every time the boat moves.

Stowage for personal gear should be sub-classified into wet and dry, hanging and folding if possible. It is sensible to make provision for wet oilskins to hang in a slim, drained locker close to the companionway and to keep them well separated from shore-going gear.

Specially shaped stowage for galley items is excellent, provided it fits the equipment of the owner's choice. Otherwise it is a waste of time and space.

All doors and drawers should be fitted with some type

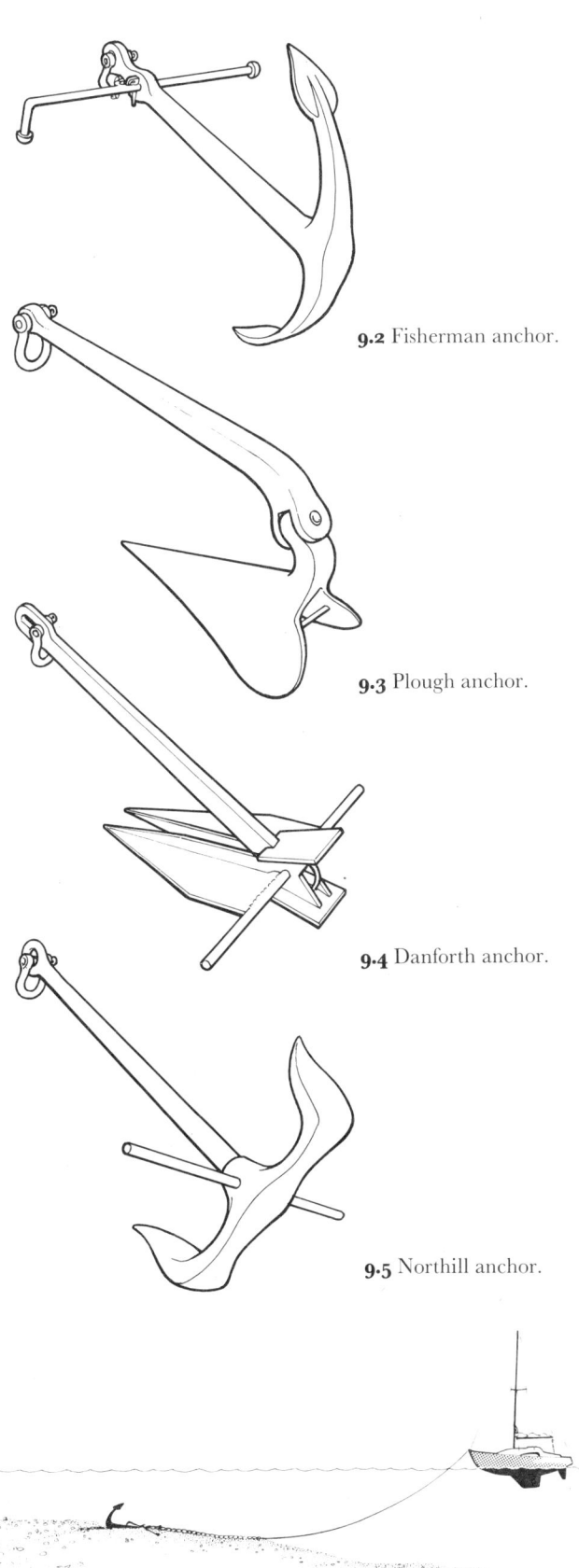

9.2 Fisherman anchor.

9.3 Plough anchor.

9.4 Danforth anchor.

9.5 Northill anchor.

An anchor well recessed into the foredeck. The drum on this boat's forestay is part of a roller reefing system for the headsail.

of catch so that they open only when required and not every time the boat heels on a new tack.

The sacrifice of stowage for extra sleeping accommodation is tolerable only in warm climates where little personal clothing is needed and where wet gear soon dries. But then, in these balmy climes it is perfectly feasible to rig a cockpit awning or tent and erect extra bunks alfresco.

Guardrails

Guardrails, their stanchions well fastened to a firm base, are necessary on any boat which ventures to sea and they must be of a suitable height to perform their duty of preventing crew members from falling overboard: lower than about 18in (half a metre), they can have quite the opposite effect and act as trip-rails.

Pulpits and aft pulpits must also be robust and well fastened. A cage is often fitted around the mast of an ocean-going yacht to hold a man securely while he is engaged in sail changing.

Deck layout

The cruising boat can benefit greatly from the labour saving deck gadgetry devised for the racing market. But that is no reason to splatter the decks indiscriminately with high-powered winches and a multiplicity of control lines. Sheeting perfection counts for little if a winch is sited just where the helmsman finds it most convenient to sit. Winch handles will accidentally be dropped overboard if they are sited a long reach from their winch – deliberately thrown overboard if in use

9.6 A length of chain between the mooring warp and the anchor helps to keep the pull on the anchor horizontal.

A high degree of luxury aboard this 30-footer (9m). Wood and
fabrics give a warm and friendly atmosphere. The saloon table
may be lowered to form a double berth; galley and navigatorium
are in the centre of the boat, for least motion, and a w.c.
compartment and hanging locker separates the fo'c's'le from the
main saloon.

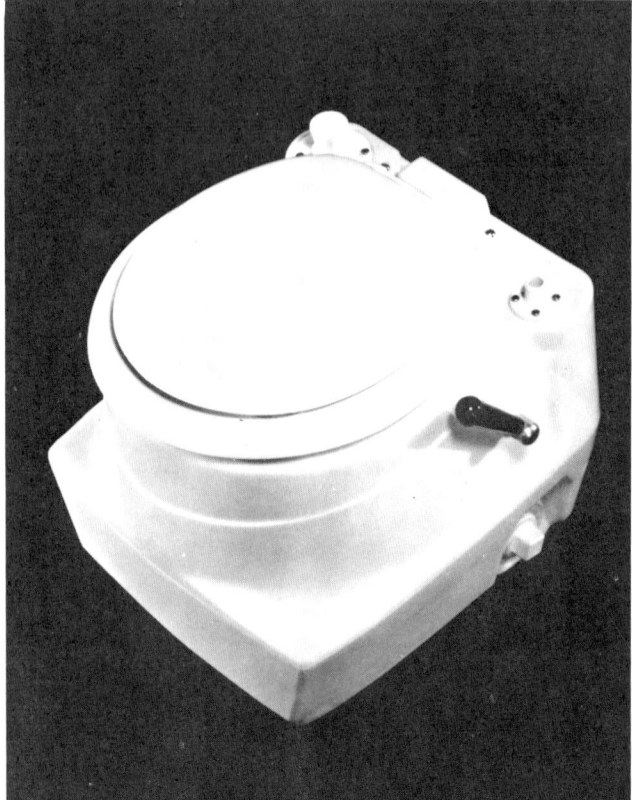

The modern chemical toilet need take no more room than the
basic 'bucket-and-chuck it' system.

the winch grinder's hand is smashed into a coaming or
another fitting.

The deck itself should be finished with an efficient
non-slip material. There are plenty on the market
without resorting to a coarse grit which will wear
through a pair of trousers in a single weekend.

Self Steering

However well balanced the boat, she will not sail round
the world on her own. The short-handed long distance
sailor may fit self-steering gear rather than risk the wind
changing direction while the tiller is lashed for long
periods. The basic steering gear consists of a vane which
swings to the wind and adjusts the angle of the rudder to
every change, to match the trim of the sails. More
complex equipment involves the use of a servo-rudder
to assist the vane in turning the boat's main steering
rudder.

Fuels

Argument rages continually over the best type of fuel to
use afloat. Proponents of the alcohol cooking stove base
their arguments on the explosive properties of gas.
Nevertheless many thousands of boat owners have
cooked on gas for many years without incident. The key
to avoiding accidental explosion is to maintain a rigid
discipline on maintaining the equipment used and on
turning off the gas supply when it is not needed. The gas
itself should if possible be stowed in a locker which
drains overboard, for cooking gas is heavier than air
and any leak will otherwise drain into the bilges and
remain undetected until spontaneous combustion results from the introduction of a spark.

Similarly, supporters of the inboard diesel engine
claim that petrol is a dangerous fuel to carry afloat.
Another argument is that a diesel donkey requires less
frequent attention than a petrol auxiliary if it is to be
totally reliable.

Fresh water should be stowed away from the light, in
a rustproof container to avoid contamination. For long
distance cruising it may be necessary to fit a secondary
plumbing system to feed salt water to the sink and w.c.

Comfort below

The cabin layout will depend on both the duties of the
boat and the degree of comfort demanded by the
owner. Double berths, electrically powered re-
frigerators, hi-fi and television are all well and good in a
marina berth but they look very silly on the high seas
when the boat is tossing and pitching and there isn't an
electricity sub-station for a thousand miles.

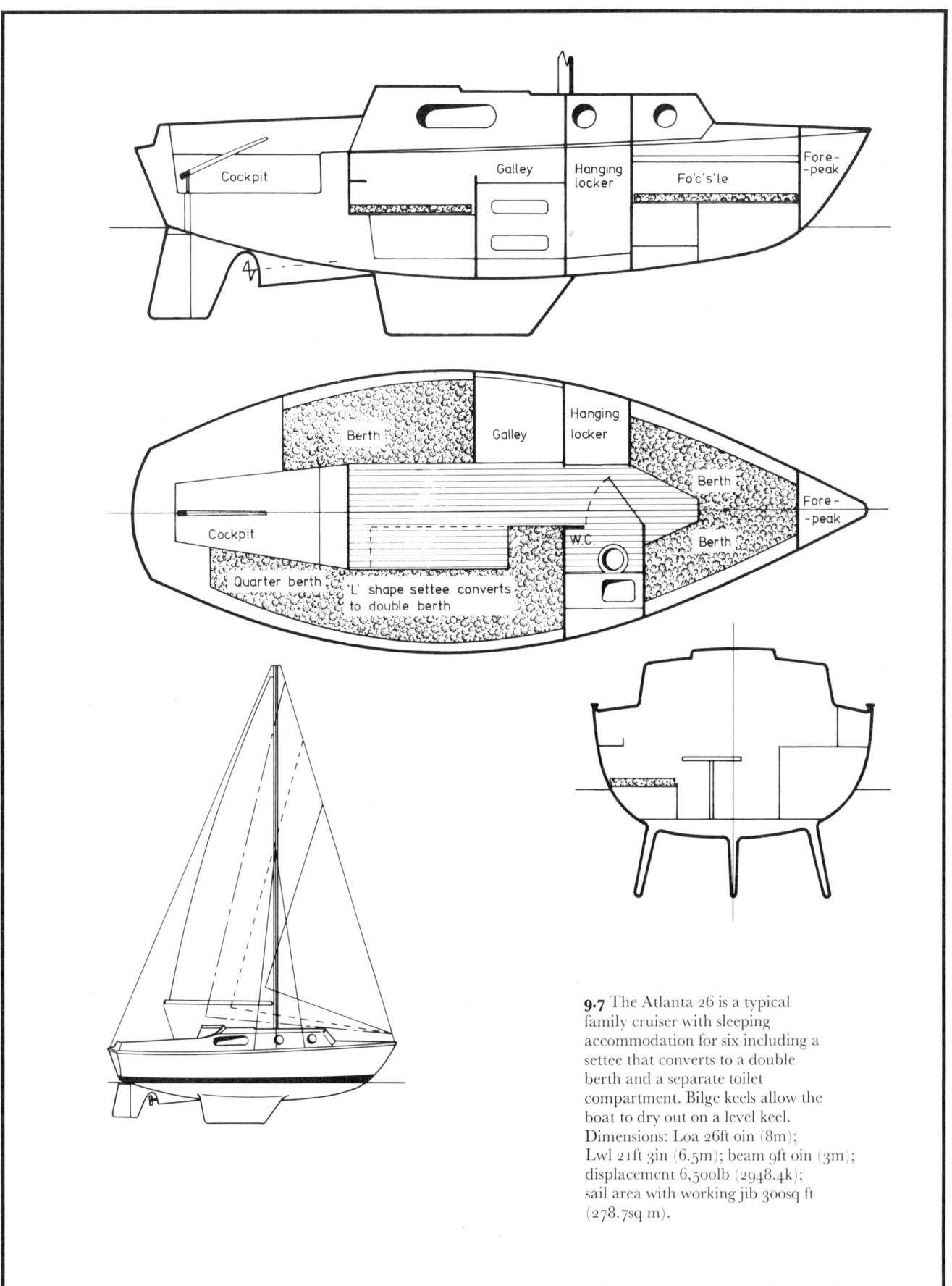

Cockpit

Galley

Hanging locker

Fo'c's'le

Fore-peak

Berth

Galley

Hanging locker

Berth

Fore-peak

Cockpit

Quarter berth

'L' shape settee converts to double berth

W.C

Berth

9·7 The Atlanta 26 is a typical family cruiser with sleeping accommodation for six including a settee that converts to a double berth and a separate toilet compartment. Bilge keels allow the boat to dry out on a level keel. Dimensions: Loa 26ft 0in (8m); Lwl 21ft 3in (6.5m); beam 9ft 0in (3m); displacement 6,500lb (2948.4k); sail area with working jib 300sq ft (278.7sq m).

Narrow bunks may look Spartan but there are none more comfortable when the boat is under way. If they are to be used at sea, they must be fitted with some form of leeboard to keep the occupant in place when the boat heels. Fabric bunk cushions look more attractive and do not reflect the extremes of heat and cold experienced on contact with p.v.c. covers. On the other hand they cannot be sponged clean so easily and if a wet oilskin is laid down carelessly, the damp patch will take a long time to dry – it may even recur as the salt which soaked into the fabric attracts moisture from the atmosphere. Children's lolipops and seasick crew members can wreak havoc on the pristine slub weave, too.

The saloon table should be fiddled, (that is, have raised edges), and be sufficiently large to accommodate at least one plate for each crew member. It is a bonus if it can be transported to an alternative position in the cockpit for alfresco meals. A good idea, too, if it incorporates bottle stowage and can be swung out of the way when not required.

Toilet compartment

The marine toilets can range from the expressively-named bucket- and chuck-it arrangement to a sumptuously equipped boudoir complete with shower. As more and more families are joining the head of the household afloat, builders are having to satisfy the demand for a 'proper toilet'.

Small chemical toilets made of plastics are ideal for the small cruiser. They require very little more space than the traditional bucket, are more stable, have a flushing facility and a separate holding tank for ease of emptying at the next port of call.

Pump-out toilets naturally require the drilling of holes in the hull – there are recorded cases of the incorrect use of the loo causing swamping and even sinking of the boat!

The toilet compartment often doubles as the 'wet' hanging locker but this is a less than perfect arrangement, particularly if a shower is fitted. Showers are becoming increasingly popular and do not add greatly to the cost of building. The compartment is supplied with a drained floor, over which a grating is fitted and the whole area becomes the shower.

Navigation

If passages are restricted to coastal hops, where each landfall is clearly within sight of the previous one, a full-scale navigatorium is pure ostentation. (It is nonetheless wise to keep a log in case a sudden sea mist should blot out the landscape). Chartwork for day cruising is often performed on the saloon table, but for reliable

The navigator's basic needs are fulfilled: a chart table which will accept his largest chart folded once, stowage for other charts underneath, a personal light and handy stowage for other navigation equipment.

navigation over a long period the navigator must be provided with a chart table of adequate size, good stowage for his charts and a comfortable, stable seat as close to the centre of the boat as practicable to minimize any motion which may encourage seasickness.

Every boat should carry a good compass, also charts and tide tables of the waters in which she is sailing. High on the list of refinements for those who sail more than a couple of miles between stops are echo sounder (unless the cruising ground is an area where the water is very deep right in to the shore), radio direction finder for locating navigation beacons and radio for receiving shipping forecasts.

Galley

Unless the crew is a long-suffering one which will not mutiny on a staple diet of potato crisp sandwiches and canned beer, something more than a knife and a mug is required in the way of galley equipment.

It *is* possible to produce an interesting hot meal on one of those single burners which screw in to a minute gas cannister, but it calls for an expert galley slave who, in different surroundings, could produce a meal of

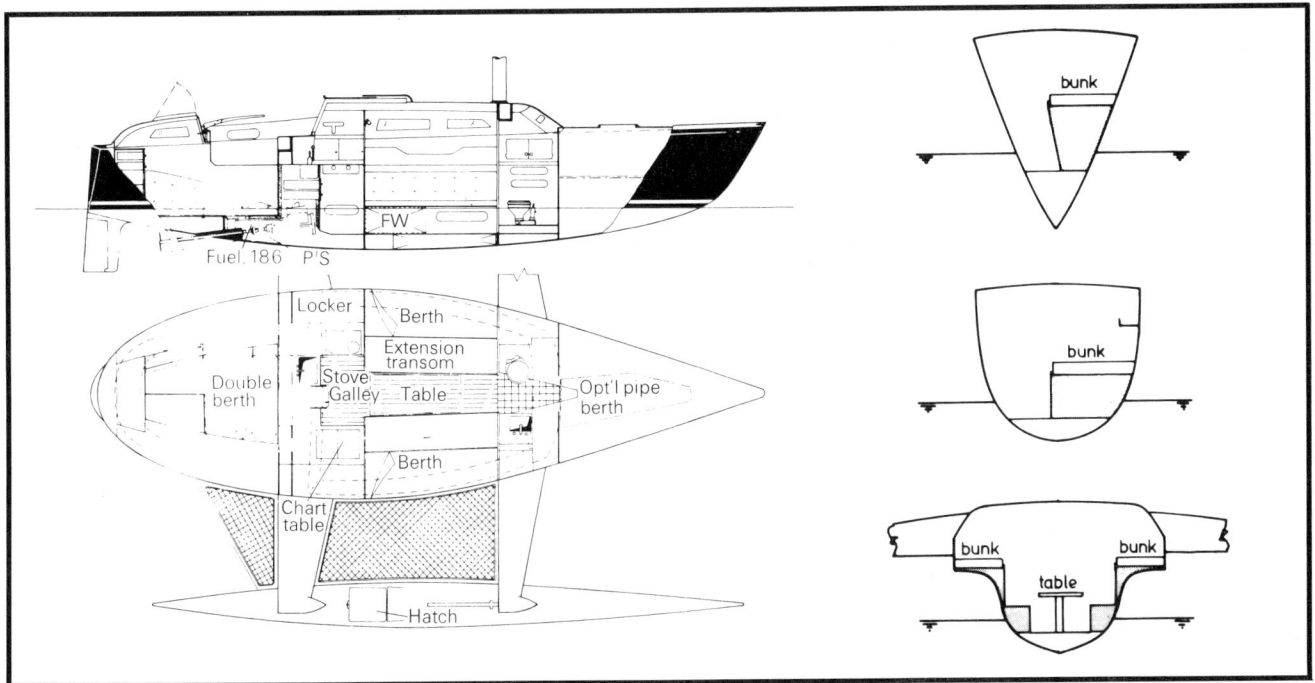

9.8a (*left*) Accommodation plan of a 33ft (10m) cruising trimaran.
9.8b (*right*) Stowage space available in different hulls.

cordon bleu standards. The single burner should be reserved for the brewing of coffee and soup aboard the mini-cruiser which makes no pretence at galley accommodation and whose crew plan to eat ashore regularly.

If a cooker is to be a permanent fixture, two rings require very little more space than one. And two rings plus a grill require very little extra depth over a basic two-ring layout.

Proper cookers with ovens are admittedly more space-consuming but well worth installing on a serious cruising boat. A stove should be gimballed, and fiddles should be available to prevent pots and pans from sliding off. If meals are to be prepared while the boat is under way, the cook can be provided with a retaining strap – just a broad webbing strap which is secured at one end and has a snap release at the other. This will provide essential support when both hands are needed for more important activities than maintaining personal balance.

Stowage and sinks should be deep and narrow, rather than shallow and wide: compare the ease of containing champagne in a proper champagne glass at a cocktail party with the amount which is spilt over all and sundry when one of those shallow, long-stalked saucer-like monstrosities is proffered.

Emergency equipment

So often one hears the term 'safety equipment' applied to flares liferafts and the like. Safety equipment is every piece of equipment on the boat, right down to the last nut and bolt. All equipment must be safely secured to safe mountings.

Flares, fire extinguishers, liferafts, pumps, radar reflectors, spare tillers and devices which bleep 'Mayday, Mayday' are emergency, not safety, equipment.

Flares must be kept dry and accessible and replaced when their due date expires; a liferaft should be capable of carrying the number of people in the normal crew; pumps should resist clogging by debris; the spare tiller should be kept handy: most of all each crew member should be drilled in the use of each item of emergency equipment.

It is sometimes claimed that the small yacht's radar reflector is of dubious value. This usually goes hand in hand with the claim that the bridge of the potential enemy is not always manned. But a radar reflector does increase the chance of a small yacht being spotted by the master of a supertanker in time to avoid a collision. If it comes into its own only once during its lifetime, it has been money well spent.

Multihulls

Accepting that there is a risk of capsize in extreme conditions, catamarans nonetheless have a lot to recommend them for cruising applications. Most can hold their own to windward against monohulls of a comparable length, while their performance off the wind can vary between slightly- to appreciably-faster. With two hulls, the opportunities to provide good accommodation are more than doubled, any narrowness of the hulls being offset by the extra space available in the bridgedeck which joins them.

Even in quite small cats, standing headroom is practicable in the hulls, although there is usually only sitting headroom under the bridgedeck, for aesthetic reasons. Cockpit and foredeck area is vast and the uprightness with which a cat deports herself makes her an ideal play area for children – given suitable netting guardrails around the ship. The absence of heeling permits the use of more domestic type saloon furniture, too, unless the cat is to cross oceans.

Trimarans on a small scale can be even more cramped than their monohull counterparts, for all the accommodation must be confined to the main hull and this often narrows sharply below the waterline, just where the conventional boat's stowage is sited. But larger tris, whose floats are sufficiently large to spread the accommodation load, are a different kettle of fish.

Multihulls will take the ground comfortably and for this reason can often benefit from the cheapness of a drying mooring in shoal water. This is often necessary to offset the sometimes punitive levy demanded of multihull visitors by some marina operators. Some trimarans have swing-wing floats, which fold alongside the main hull when at rest for the same reason.

10 Understanding the weather

To the sailing man, weather means two important things: wind and visibility. He cares little if it rains and soaks the family wash or if endless weeks of sunshine dry up the carefully tended lawns of semi-detached suburbia. But he must know the expected strength of the wind which he will encounter when he goes afloat – and whether mist or fog will render his passage difficult or dangerous.

Unfortunately the weather forecasters of the popular media seldom present their information with the same sense of priorities, so the serious yachtsman must make some effort to understand the workings of the weather systems and to become an avid follower of the specialised shipping forecasts. Even these are restricted to quite a brief period of air time and it is necessary to be familiar with the verbal shorthand used to convey the up-to-date message.

There are those who understand weather maps and those who never will and they will often be found sailing side by side in the same type of boat. But it is the skipper who has the ability to read the changes in the sky and confirm or deny the day's forecast who will have the edge on his companion. If cruising, he will shorten sail before the wind increases to such a pitch that the manoeuvre becomes uncomfortable and difficult. If racing, he may be able to tack off and pick up a new breeze while Mr Don't Know is becalmed.

Wind is moving air and it is moving air which dictates the world's weather patterns. Warm air rises over the tropics, cold air sinks over the poles, but the straightforward movement of air between the two is complicated by the fact that the major land masses are adjacent to seas of contrasting temperatures. Moreover, exchanges of heat on such a scale produce repercussions throughout the depth of atmosphere so that, at any one time, air which is cold near the surface may be relatively warm aloft and vice versa. Fortunately, the nightmare complexity of vertical temperature structure can be summarised by one very useful factor at the surface: the pressure which that depth of atmosphere exerts. Pressure varies from day to day and from place to place, but if values at any one moment are plotted on to a map in the appropriate situations, they give a pressure contour picture just like a geographical contour map. Lines called isobars can be drawn joining places having equal pressure and these form closed concentric patterns round centres of high and low pressure. The pressure readings are made strictly comparable by adding to each the pressure of an imaginary column of air equivalent to the physical height above sea-level at which the readings are made.

Like a river which must run downhill, air tries to move from a high-level contour line to a low-level one but its journey is deflected by the spinning of the earth so the air actually moves at right angles to the anticipated direction; that is, it moves parallel to the isobars on the weather map. This assumes no disturbance by surface friction, hence a level of 2,000ft (609m) is taken to be the norm.

In the Northern Hemisphere the wind at 2,000ft (609m) blows parallel to the isobars so that, when blowing on one's back, low pressure is on the left hand. This means it blows anti-clockwise round low pressure and clockwise round high pressure.

The reverse is true of the Southern Hemisphere: with the wind on one's back, low pressure is on the right hand. Wind blows clockwise round low pressure and anti-clockwise round high pressure.

But boats have sails, not wings, so the wind at 2,000ft (609m) is purely of academic interest to the yachtsman. The drag of friction at the surface prevents the full 90° deflection of air from the high-to-low direction. The deflection at the surface is more like 60° over the land and about 80° over the sea.

In the Northern Hemisphere surface wind is backed from the wind at 2,000ft (609m) by about 30° over the land and about 10° over the sea. In the Southern Hemisphere it is veered by the same amount.

Beaufort Wind Scale

Beaufort No.	Velocity in knots	Description	Sea state
0	Less than 1	Calm	Sea like a mirror.
1	1–3	Light air	Ripples with the appearance of scales are formed but without foam crests.
2	4–6	Light breeze	Small wavelets, still short but more pronounced. Crests have a glassy appearance and do not break.
3	7–10	Gentle breeze	Large wavelets. Crests begin to break. Foam of glassy appearance. Perhaps scattered white horses.
4	11–16	Moderate breeze	Small waves, becoming longer, fairly frequent white horses.
5	17–21	Fresh breeze	Moderate waves taking a more pronounced long form; many white horses are formed. Chance of some spray.
6	22–27	Strong breeze	Large waves begin to form; the white foam crests are more extensive everywhere. Probably some spray.
7	28–33	Near gale	Sea heaps up, and white foam from breaking waves begins to be blown in streaks along the direction of the wind.
8	34–40	Gale	Moderately high waves of greater length; edges of crests begin to break into spindrift. The foam is blown in well-marked streaks along the direction of the wind.
9	41–47	Strong gale	High waves. Dense streaks of foam along the direction of the wind. Crests of waves begin to topple, tumble and roll over. Spray may affect visibility.
10	48–55	Storm	Very high waves with long, overhanging crests. The resulting foam in great patches is blown in dense white streaks along the direction of the wind. On the whole the surface of the sea takes a white appearance. The tumbling of the sea becomes heavy and shocklike. Visibility affected.
11	56–63	Violent storm	Exceptionally high waves. (Small and medium-sized ships might be lost to view behind the waves.) The sea is completely covered with long white patches of foam lying along the direction of the wind. Everywhere the edges of the wave crests are blown into froth. Visibility affected.
12	64 +	Hurricane	The air is filled with foam and spray. Sea completely white with driving spray; visibility very seriously affected.

In both hemispheres this gives the result that surface air flows in towards the centres of a low-pressure circulation – a depression – and outwards from the centre of a high-pressure circulation – an anti-cyclone. Friction slows up surface wind speed by about 30% over the land but by rather less over the sea. However, there is usually enough vertical movement of air to bring down to the surface from higher levels momentary gusts of wind with speeds and direction more like those at 2,000ft (609m) level.

The strength of the wind at 2,000ft (609m) can be gauged from the distance between the isobars – the closer together, the stronger the wind.

The biggest shortcoming of the isobaric chart is that it shows the picture at only one moment, whereas weather is changing continually. However, the isobars arrange themselves in certain classic patterns which indicate a fairly standard type of weather sequence. Those who can recognize these patterns are half way to being able to predict the weather that will follow.

Anticyclones are sluggish systems, slow to establish themselves by persistent but gradual rise in pressure, often reluctant to depart and they decorate the weather charts with widely spaced isobars, often arranged asymetrically. The charts tend to look empty and thermals grow only to shallow heights because the outflow of air near the ground causes air above the centre to subside and warm. The weather is fine in summer but foggy or frosty in winter and pressure winds are often maddeningly light. Sailing becomes difficult on rivers, lakes and reservoirs inland but coastal sailors are better off because of seabreezes.

Wind direction may change in haphazard fashion as the pattern re-orientates itself, but the difficulty of forecasting such a change should not constitute a danger, because the wind is light. Strong pressure wind does occur in fine, anticyclonic weather, but usually in the bordering *ridge of high pressure* between the centre of the anticyclone and a deepening depression elsewhere.

It is the passage of *depressions* which gives wind troubles to yachtsmen, not only because of the risk of gales, but because of the changing wind directions as well. The particular nightmare in relatively confined waters is that a safe windward shore can suddenly become a dangerous leeward shore from which it is not possible to escape.

There are two broad types of depression pattern. First the busy, almost circular, pattern of closely spaced isobars which indicates an active, travelling depression. It has probably been born along the boundary between two air masses, and the circulation carries with it a wave of contrasting air and well-marked surface fronts. The depression announces its approach in the sky by the flat sheet cloud of a warm front, and confirms its

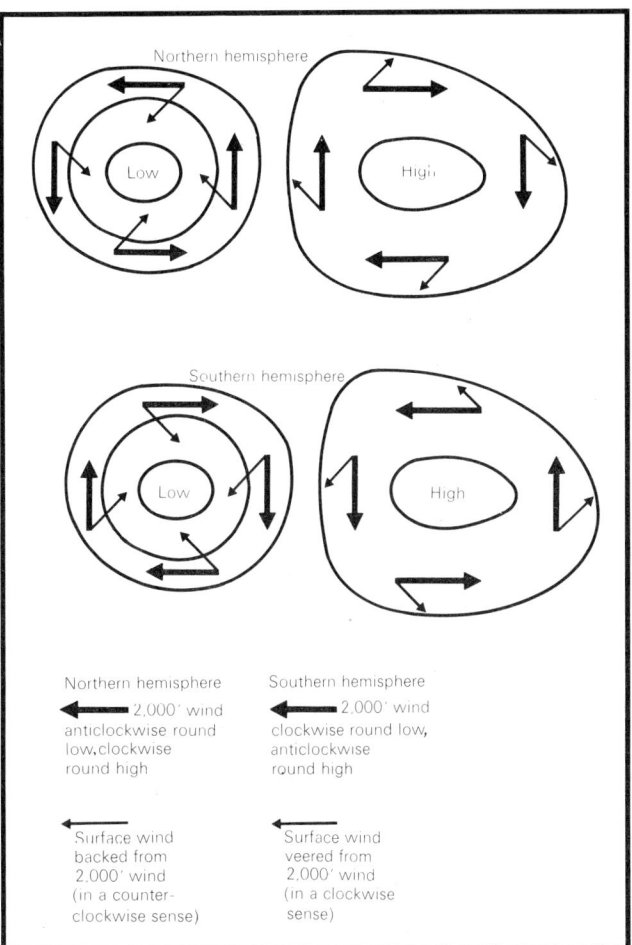

10.1 Direction of airflow at the surface and at 2,000ft (609.6m) above ground around centres of pressure, northern and southern hemispheres.

progress by a message on every barometer along its line of approach. Pressure starts to fall at a rate commensurate with the speed of approach of the depression, proximity to the path of the centre, and the rate at which the system itself is deepening. Pressure always falls more quickly at the centre than on the periphery, leading to a steeper pressure gradient, more isobars on the chart, and more wind in the boat's sails. *Rapidly falling pressure* ahead of warm front cloud, and *rapidly rising pressure* behind the cold front as the depression passes indicate a risk of *gales*.

Figure 10.3 shows how these warnings also indicate changes in wind direction. The abrupt manner in which the isobars change direction at the warm and cold fronts is not artistic licence, but an indication of real fact. Assuming a boat is on the same side of the depression centre as the fronts, the following rules apply:

Northern hemisphere: Pressure falls, and wind backs ahead of the warm front. Pressure steadies, and wind veers behind the warm front. Pressure rises, and wind veers still further behind the cold front.

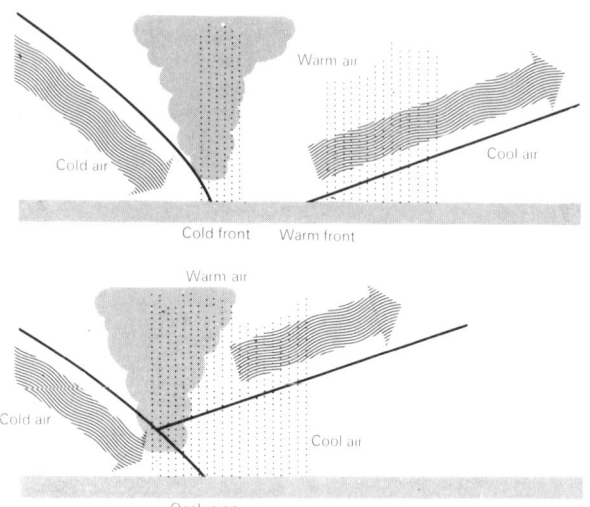

10.2 Cross sections through a typical cold front (*top left*), warm front (*top right*) and occlusion (*bottom*).

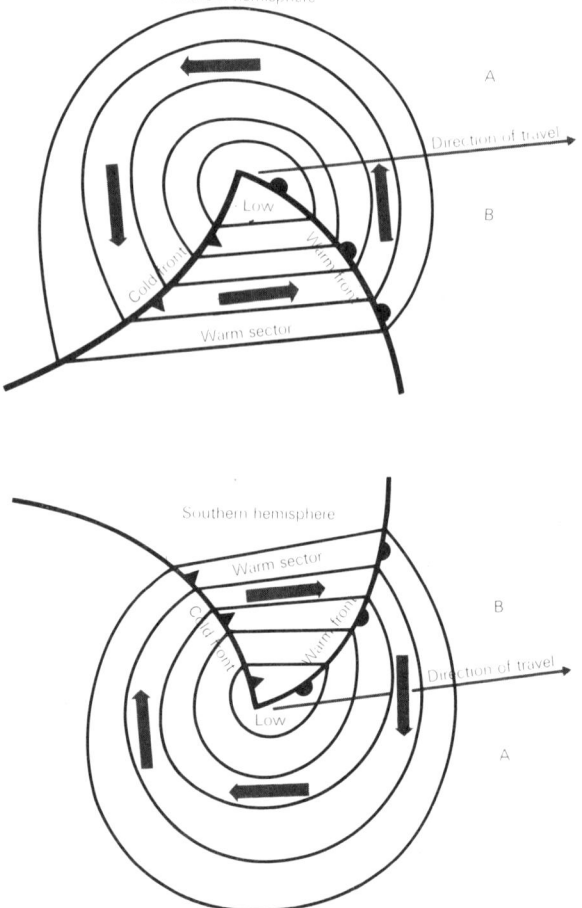

10.3 Manner of wind change as depressions pass overhead, northern and southern hemispheres. Changeable usually unpleasant weather results when depressions pass overhead.

Southern hemisphere: Pressure falls, and wind veers ahead of the warm front. Pressure steadies, and wind backs behind the warm front. Pressure rises, and wind backs still further behind the cold front.

If a boat is on the opposite side of the path of the centre from the fronts, wind direction changes from the one extreme to the other but in the opposite manner. Hence the importance of knowing your position relative to the travelling centre so that you can make a reasonable estimate whether a nearby shore will be to windward or to leeward.

Cyclones, hurricanes and typhoons are all names of low-pressure circulations of greater violence, though smaller cross-section area, than depressions. They occur over subtropical seas, feed on a diet of warm, moist air, and generally revert to ordinary depressions once they reach land. No one in their senses would want to be anywhere near a hurricane, but for those who unfortunately find themselves in the vicinity, the wind follows the same directional behaviour as in depressions. Wind blows in almost circular fashion, perhaps as strong as 200mph near the centre, but at the centre there is a relatively calm 'eye' where wind drops to about 10-15mph. It affords a brief respite to effect repairs or batten down more securely, but the wind always returns just as fiercely – although from the opposite direction.

After a brief maturity active depressions start to wane, central pressure rises, pressure gradients decrease, and wind drops. The depression drifts or grinds to a halt, and by that time the pressure pattern has changed. The centre will have travelled faster than the outer edge where the cold front may be trailing behind and becoming extinct. Near the centre the cold front will have overtaken the warm front and lifted the warm sector off the ground, at which stage the fronts are said to be *occluded*. The weather chart may look as empty of isobars as in an anti-cyclone, but there is one important difference. Surface winds, being backed from those at 2,000ft, blow slightly inwards towards the centre of the depression, and this convergence forces air above the centre to lift and become cooled. Cloud and rain may therefore continue, particularly if the isobars change direction in strongly marked fashion and bring together airs of contrasting nature. Such a V of isobars is called a trough, and when it is as extreme as that shown in figure 10.4, makes the pattern look as insecure as a stretched water drop about to separate from a dripping tap, and that is precisely the danger. The area becomes the possible birth-place of another depression which may make a take-over bid from the parent depression. Forecasters can only stress the probability of this happening; they cannot pinpoint the actual centre until it has formed or a vital clue is reported by which time, if

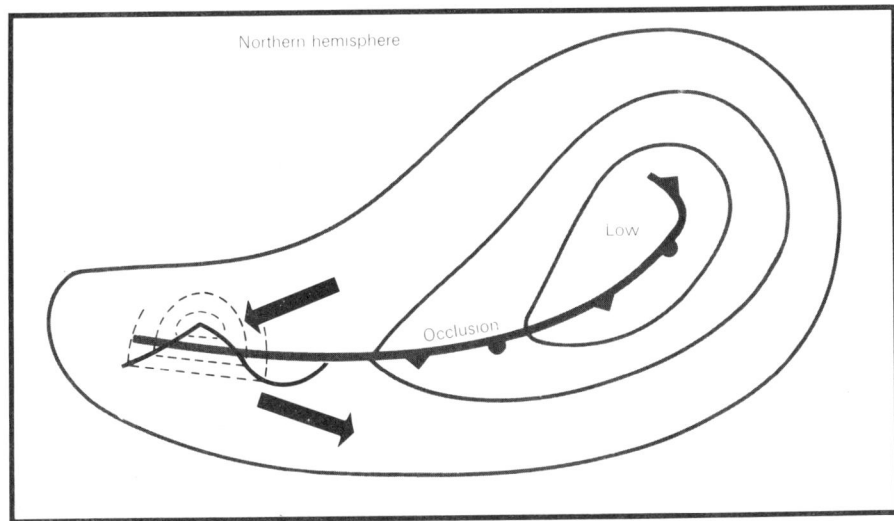

10.4 Filling depression and trailing occlusion liable to wave and generate another depression.

you are sailing in the vicinity, weather may deteriorate with little warning. Always distrust a sloppy-looking depression with troughing isobars, and watch carefully for cloud and barometer clues for the formation of a secondary depression.

Condensation

Clouds often serve as tell-tale indicators. *All air contains water vapour*, even on a clear day. The supply is obtained by evaporation from the seas, rivers and lakes of the world and the specially moist airstreams are those which have had a long journey over the sea. But at any particular temperature air has a maximum capacity for this invisible water vapour, and the capacity decreases as temperature falls. *Dew-point* is the level at which air is full to the brim with vapour. Any further reduction in temperature results in condensation – dew, mist, fog, cloud, rain, or snow. The moister the air, the greater the risk of these forms of visible weather with even small falls in temperature. It is therefore important to understand how natural cooling occurs.

Cooling by contact

(1) Air may cool because a cloudless sky allows heat to radiate away from the ground into space. When there is little or no pressure wind to stir up this cooling, the cold, heavy air squats low on level surfaces, or drains by gravity down slopes into hollows. Any cooling beyond dew-point results first in *dew* (as on the outside of a jug of iced water taken from the refrigerator into a warm room), and later, as cooling is transferred through a greater depth of air, in *mist or fog*. A hot summer sun will clear all of these over land next day, but they often persist throughout the day in winter.

(2) A moving airstream cools when it journeys over

colder surfaces, for instance when a mild airstream suddenly gains precedence after a bitterly cold winter. Indoors the air blooms as dew over cold furniture in unheated rooms. Outdoors fog forms temporarily over snow surfaces until the snow itself melts in the warm air, but this takes time. *Sea fog* occurs when an airstream cools over a particularly cold sea current, or when it travels into progressively colder latitudes. The longer the sea track taken by the airstream, the more moisture it will have acquired *en route*, and the more rapidly will dew-point be approached, with the danger of fog. If wind is fairly strong, fog may be lifted off the surface to form, instead, a low ceiling of grey formless cloud called *stratus*. Because the temperature of the sea surface changes only imperceptibly during any one day, it requires a radical change in airstream before sea fog or stratus over the sea clear. The sun alone has little chance of doing it. Over land, however, a hot sun will burn off any sea fog or stratus which drifts onshore

Sun almost obscured by warm front sheet cloud. Rain imminent.

Sea fog drifting across a shore line in summer. One mile inland there is bright sunshine. *Ingrid Holdford*

during the summer. Sea fog or stratus can occur even during a heat-wave if the airstream is particularly moist, but evasive action is possible if local geography permits. Search for a length of coastline which is in the lee of a sizeable headland over which the airstream can dry out, and you may find bright sunshine although there is thick fog only a few miles upwind.

Cloud

When air is lifted above the ground, the column of air above it becomes less, and it therefore suffers a reduction of atmospheric pressure, expands, and thereby cools. This is why a soda-syphon cartridge becomes so exceedingly cold once the compressed air inside has been released into the syphon. To understand cloud formation, therefore, means looking for the methods by which air is lifted into regions of reduced pressure.

(1) Air lifts and cools when it is forced to surmount *hills or mountains*. This often causes a cloud to form over a mountain top when the sky nearby is clear, or it produces a lower cloud base over the mountain than already exists nearby.

(2) Air lifts in *thermal upcurrents*. Air near the ground warms, rises, is replaced by air from above which warms in turn, rises, etc., etc. – a continuous process leading to a rising air current. In this thermal air cools at known fixed rates. The air mass in which the thermal

is rising has a vertical temperature pattern which is a reflection of its previous history, and varies each day. Air in the thermal may, therefore, have a different temperature from the surroundings in which it is rising, but so long as it is warmer than the surroundings, the thermal air will be buoyant and continue to soar. On days when the air mass is particularly cold aloft (e.g. of polar origin, but moving towards the Equator) thermals may reach several miles high. When the air mass is relatively warm aloft (e.g. air moving from somewhere in the region of the Equator towards the poles), cooling air in the thermal soon meets a lid of air warmer than itself, and it rises no more. The strongest thermals occur over land in spring and summer during the daytime. When the sun sets, thermals cease. Thermals also occur when cold air travels over a sea, and in that case thermals may continue into the night because sea-surface temperature does not change.

At some point in the upward journey of a thermal air cools beyond dew-point and the base of a cloud forms. Condensation continues in the thermal and produces a *cumulus* cloud with a crisp billowing top. If thermals are shallow, cumulus remains no more than modest tufts of fleece. If thermals are deep, towering castles in the air called *cumulonimbus* develop, which gives showers of rain, snow or hail, sometimes with a dramatic accompaniment of thunder and lightening. That alone can be a hazardous weather deterioration, but the disturbance

She would have set cotton sails for at least the first fifty years of her life, but now she is resplendent in a new suit of terylenes: 'Urchin', built in the late 1800s, is thought to be the oldest boat on England's Lake Windermere. *John Watney*

Crew drill on the forward set of ratlines aboard 'Tectona'. *John Watney*

Rolling . . . not down to Rio but down the Solent in a stiff breeze. Arthur Slater's 'Prospect of Whitby', spinnaker drawing and mainsail well reefed, makes the most of the conditions. The jib has been lowered in favour of a tallboy, a high aspect, narrow sail which is used to improve the flow of wind between the slot formed by spinnaker and mainsail.

John Watney

'Marionette' owned by Chris Dunning, captain of England's Admiral's Cup team in 1977.
Silvio Mursia

These cumulonimbus contain showers, perhaps hail, thunder and lightening; near their base changeable winds will occur.

Cumulus forms over mountains because of intense heating over slopes facing the sun and because air must surmount any obstacle.

Cumulus over land is accompanied by an offshore wind which causes cumulus clouds to drift over the sea.

Cumulus over land are being held back from drifting across the sea because of a sea breeze blowing on shore.

Small cumulus spread over the sky; effect of river is insignificant as its area is comparatively small. *Ingrid Holford*

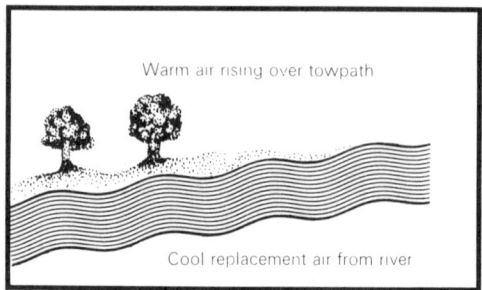

10.5 River zephyrs.

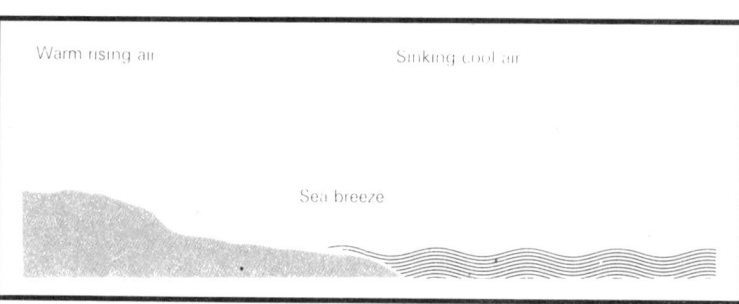

10.6 Sea breezes.

of wind in the vicinity of such a cloud is of much greater importance to boats afloat. A cumulonimbus replenishes its violent upcurrents by sucking in air from below like a giant vacuum cleaner, and a yachtsman must prepare for wild fluctuations of surface wind, both in direction and speed. Do not be lulled by any impression that the cloud, previously travelling towards you, is now travelling away. A cumulonimbus has no reversing gear and it travels on the pressure wind of the day, but it has an abundance of power with which to take temporary control over surface wind.

(3) Air lifts into regions of lower atmospheric pressure when two air masses of different temperature and humidity characteristics confront each other from different directions. They cannot mix together at once, and as a temporary expedient, cold air undercuts warm air, giving violent upcurrents and a line of showers at the surface boundary called the *cold front*. Warm air, pushed by cold air, may be forced to slither upwards over cool air ahead, giving a more extensive sheet of *flat cloud*. It starts as a thin veil of high ice cloud, which gradually obscures the sun, and thickens to a solid looking grey, without the characteristic billows of a cumulus cloud. At that stage rain starts to fall and

continues for several hours until the arrival of the surface boundary called the *warm front*, after which rain ceases. These clouds bear messages to the yachtsman about the future behaviour of the main pressure winds.

Gusts and shifts

The inshore and inland sailor will meet many more gusts, calms and windshifts than the skipper who ventures offshore. The inland sailor, especially, becomes very adept at threading his way through barely perceptible zephyrs on a day of apparently total calm.

Most of these gusts are caused by the topography of the landscape or architecture in the immediate vicinity. Wind striking a row of warehouses or trees on a river bank, for example, will either have to climb over the obstruction or find a path around it. Hence quite strong gusts can be experienced as wind is funnelled down a road or path leading to a river bank or sea shore.

There can be some unexpected and useful gusts, too, in the lee of a high dam wall of a reservoir as the wind passing across it forms back-eddies. Normally any form of barrier – even quite a sparse scattering of trees and bushes – to windward of a stretch of sailing water should be regarded with suspicion for the turbulence it causes.

Sea breeze

The sea breeze is a shallow wind which blows from the sea to replace air rising over the land on a sunny day. It builds up gradually as the sun rises and at its peak may extend 30-40 miles (48-64 km) inland. It dies down as the sun lowers in the sky. When conditions are suitable for cumulus development over the land, the sea breeze keeps the clouds tidily above the coastline.

If the day's wind has been offshore there will certainly be a period of calm as the new sea breeze battles for supremacy over the dying offshore breeze. It may be for only a matter of minutes, but it can last for an agonizing period during which sailing boats and their crews are powerless, just drifting under the sun and waiting for some means of propulsion. Then suddenly the sea breeze fills in, gently at first but soon

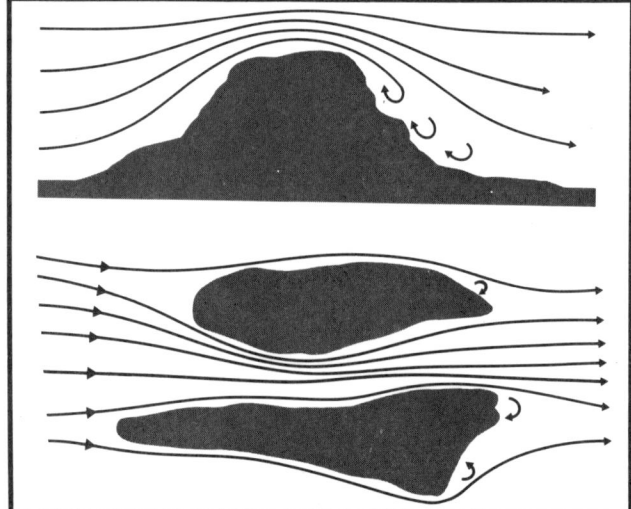

10.7 *Top* Wind increasing in speed over the top of a mountain.
Bottom Wind increasing in speed between two mountains.

building up strength until it reaches perhaps 15 knots.

A seabreeze which arises from a calm or which has to overcome an offshore breeze seldom reaches a force which need worry the average sailor. However, a sea breeze which merely augments an existing onshore breeze can build up to a wind which will be of frightening velocity to a novice.

Line squall

The line squall can hold terror for the small boat sailor. A mass of dark cloud appears to windward – usually with ample warning for the novice and the fair-weather sailor to run for shelter. On its approach the wind will increase sharply and will often be accompanied by thunder showers. The squall may last as long as half an hour before sweeping on its way, leaving a trail of capsized boats, broken masts and shivering crews. In its wake the wind will drop but will be veered from its original direction.

Beaufort Wind Scale no 3: Large wavelets. Crests begin to break. Foam of glassy appearance. Perhaps scattered white horses. *Ian Gilchrist*.

Pulpits, stanchions and guardrails must be robust and securely
mounted to the boat! *Ajax News Photos*

11 A history of ocean racers

The first yacht race can be traced back to the mid-1600s, shortly after the word yacht itself was introduced to the English language. The English king Charles II was presented with a sailing boat by the Dutch East India Company and in this he spent much time pleasure sailing. Other English noblemen followed the king's lead and this élite band of men held impromptu races on the River Thames.

It was a hundred years later that the first clubs were formed for yacht owners: by now there were many pleasure craft on the River Thames and so the Cumberland Sailing Society, named after the Duke of Cumberland, came into being to co-ordinate their competitive activities. The now-fashionable yachting mecca of Cowes had to wait until 1812 for its first yacht club, which during the 1820s became the Royal Yacht Squadron as it is known today and which formulated the first racing rules.

But during the nineteenth century every club had its own rules, few of which were enforceable. Most competitions relied on owners behaving in a gentlemanly manner towards each other. (Those who have noted the standard of rule observance at starts and round turning marks on some of today's crowded courses may be forgiven for wondering whether this is still the case.)

The Royal Alfred Yacht Club took the initiative in 1872 by appointing a measurer, producing a set of rules and insisting that yachts racing under its aegis obtain a measurement certificate. It could not be said that the adoption of these rules was universal, so the Royal Alfred went one further, circularizing all interested parties with a suggestion that all yachts should be required to present a certificate of measurement prior to racing. This at last had an effect and precipitated the formation of the embryo Yacht Racing Association – later to become the UK's national authority, the Royal Yachting Association.

Even the YRA did not have a smooth passage: its early work on the production of a set of rules was met with hostility from a handful of the leading clubs which began to toe the party line only after a studied boycott of one of those clubs' (the Royal Yacht Squadron) regattas, after which catastrophe the RYS committee, hence policy towards the YRA, was changed.

Early British rating rules were phrased along the lines of those which governed the measurement of trading ships. Deep holds were *de rigeur* in the traders, so deep, increasingly narrow, hence heavily ballasted hulls became the fashionable shape for racing yachts. Plank-on-edge, they were nicknamed, and some designers reached such extremes that their brainchildren verged on the unseaworthy. By contrast American yacht designers had already produced a wealth of fast schooners of relatively beamy hull form and light displacement, developed from the fast fishermen and pilot cutters of the Eastern Seaboard.

Despite receiving a thrashing at the hands of the schooner 'America' when she visited British waters in 1851 – and at the hands of her successors during challenges for the America's Cup which resulted from the confrontation – British designers persisted with their narrow, heavy displacement yachts.

Design development followed quite different schools of thought on both sides of the Atlantic until well after the First World War, when the Cruising Club of America adopted a rule which in essence was similar to that of the British Royal Ocean Racing Club – but the two soon followed diverging courses again, until truly international offshore racing became a reality in the 60s and all major yacht racing countries agreed an International Offshore Rule in principle.

The IOR was introduced in 1970 and has been subject to frequent modification to eliminate loopholes, to assist boats to stay competitive and to dissuade designers from going to unseaworthy extremes in their quest for victory.

It has encouraged a rather stereotyped, full-

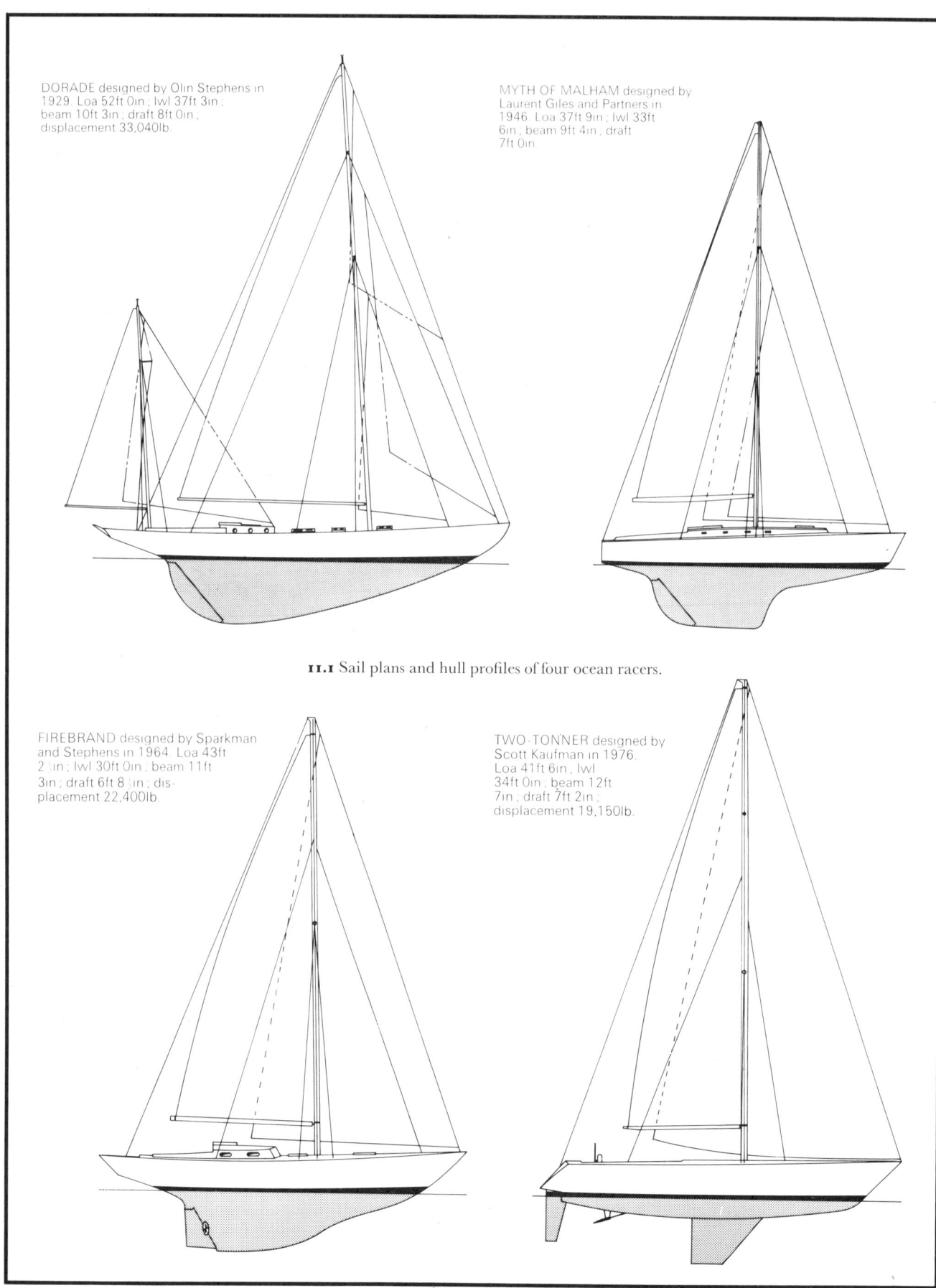

DORADE designed by Olin Stephens in
1929. Loa 52ft 0in ; lwl 37ft 3in ;
beam 10ft 3in ; draft 8ft 0in ;
displacement 33,040lb.

MYTH OF MALHAM designed by
Laurent Giles and Partners in
1946. Loa 37ft 9in ; lwl 33ft
6in ; beam 9ft 4in ; draft
7ft 0in.

11.1 Sail plans and hull profiles of four ocean racers.

FIREBRAND designed by Sparkman
and Stephens in 1964. Loa 43ft
2 in ; lwl 30ft 0in ; beam 11ft
3in ; draft 6ft 8 in ; displacement 22,400lb.

TWO-TONNER designed by
Scott Kaufman in 1976.
Loa 41ft 6in ; lwl
34ft 0in ; beam 12ft
7in ; draft 7ft 2in ;
displacement 19,150lb.

sectioned, high freeboard hull with high aspect ratio masthead rig totally different from the long-keeled moderates of the 50s and 60s. To the relief of owners of these out-rated, if not out-dated yachts, the IOR Mark III(a) was introduced to rule leniently on the features which were encouraged by older rules, so that racing boats in their dotage could continue to compete against the new, purpose-built machines.

The existence of any measurement rule brings the temptation to the designer to exploit it. In a one-design class there can be only a few millimetres difference between one boat and the next, but any rule whose purpose is to measure each and every yacht for an individual handicap rating must necessarily define certain measurement points. It is the exaggeration at these points of the dimensions which are favoured under the rule which produces a certain style of boat for a certain rule, hence the 'RORC type' or the 'IOR type' – a type, note, which the designer feels has the best rating for a given rule: not necessarily the fastest shape for a given overall length.

There is every chance that the present interest in one-

Offshore racers, 50s and 60s style, still enjoy competitive racing among themselves – and the Mark IIIa IOR has been introduced to enable them to hold their own against modern boats, too.
Trevor Davies

Flush decks, for reduced windage, are the norm on modern offshore racing boats. *Alastair Black*

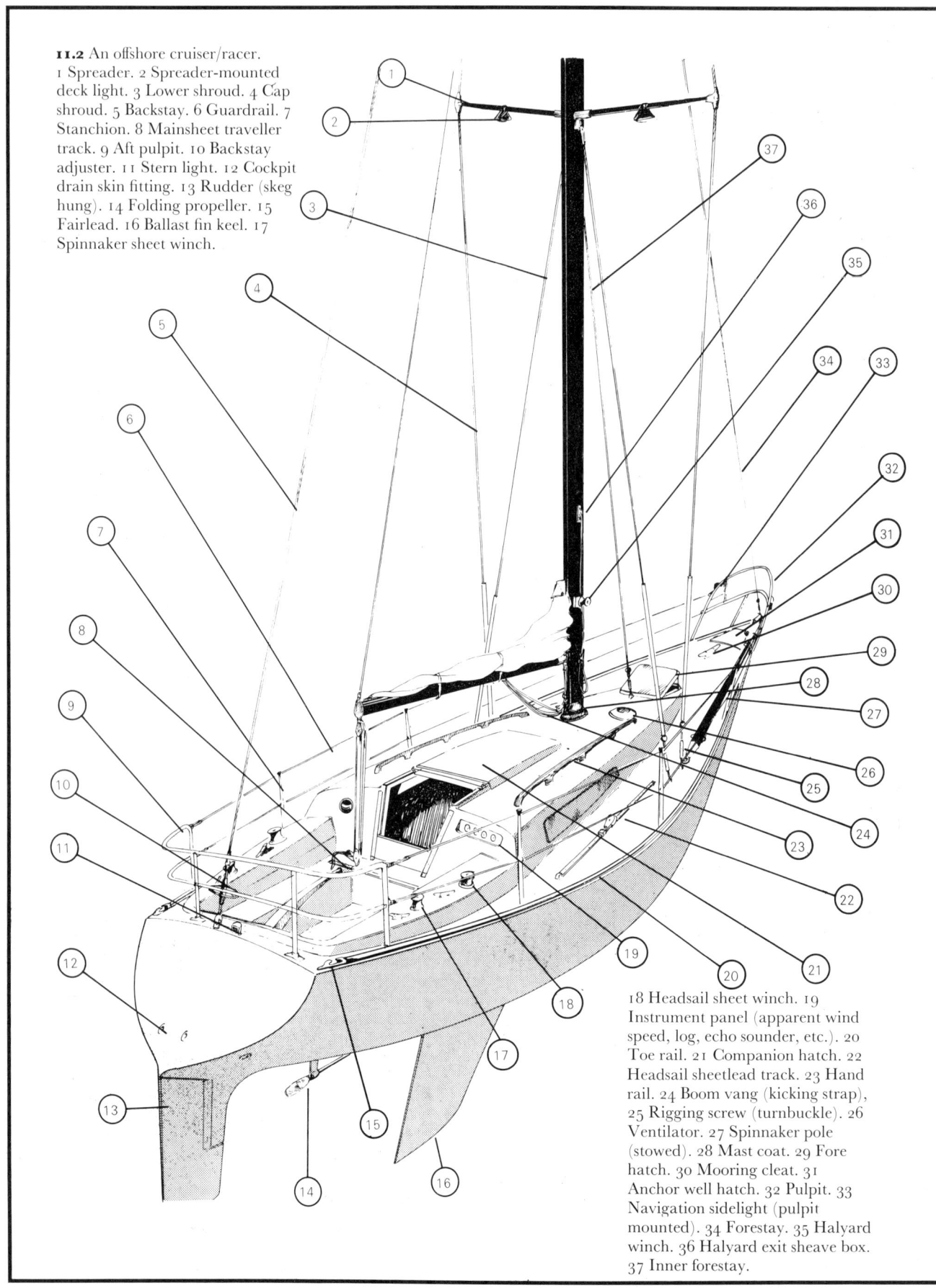

11.2 An offshore cruiser/racer.
1 Spreader. 2 Spreader-mounted deck light. 3 Lower shroud. 4 Cap shroud. 5 Backstay. 6 Guardrail. 7 Stanchion. 8 Mainsheet traveller track. 9 Aft pulpit. 10 Backstay adjuster. 11 Stern light. 12 Cockpit drain skin fitting. 13 Rudder (skeg hung). 14 Folding propeller. 15 Fairlead. 16 Ballast fin keel. 17 Spinnaker sheet winch.

18 Headsail sheet winch. 19 Instrument panel (apparent wind speed, log, echo sounder, etc.). 20 Toe rail. 21 Companion hatch. 22 Headsail sheetlead track. 23 Hand rail. 24 Boom vang (kicking strap), 25 Rigging screw (turnbuckle). 26 Ventilator. 27 Spinnaker pole (stowed). 28 Mast coat. 29 Fore hatch. 30 Mooring cleat. 31 Anchor well hatch. 32 Pulpit. 33 Navigation sidelight (pulpit mounted). 34 Forestay. 35 Halyard winch. 36 Halyard exit sheave box. 37 Inner forestay.

Spritsail barges used to be a common sight around the coasts of England, carrying all manner of cargo from coal to haystacks. Their shallow draft made them ideally suited for working the shoal waters of the East Coast and, despite their immense size, they were worked by only a man and a boy – and often their dog. The 'boy', incidentally, could be as much as seventy years of age. Now the barges which remain are being restored lovingly; as homes, as charter boats and as racing boats. There are at least half a dozen matches in the bargeman's calendar each year.
John Watney

The Uffa Fox-designed Flying Fifteen is 20ft (6m) overall and named for its waterline length. Still very popular as a family day-racer, many husband and wife crews may be found competing regularly. *John Watney*

Thirty-five knots of wind on a cold day: well, would you look happy? *John Watney*

One of the delights of cruising is to discard oilskins at the end of the day and gather round a plate of locally caught seafood in a cosy cabin, to yarn the night away over a bottle of cheering brew.
John Watney

The M & W-designed 'Vanguard' is a typical, but by not means extreme, Two Tonner under the International Offshore Rule. She was the top performer in Hong Kong's 1977 Admiral's Cup team.
Studio 77

design offshore racing will bring a new type of yacht into being, one which is fast, aesthetically pleasing and comfortable for cruising, too.

The idea of an offshore one-design has been gathering momentum for a couple of years, some trials have been held and some classes are finding favour with owners. In the USA the New York Yacht Club is supporting class racing for the Peterson designed NY40s, while in the UK the Royal Ocean Racing Club is offering to lay on separate starts for OD classes. In Scandinavia the Elvström/Kjaerulff 101 is finding favour – in Britain, too, this shows signs of becoming one of the more popular one-designs. While the US supporters are going for 40-footers (12m), in the UK those closely concerned with the concept are reckoning that offshore ODs with an upper limit of about 34ft (10m) will find most favour with owners: over that size

the financial outlay – the very thing which prevents them from joining the specialized one-off circus – would prove a deterrent.

It is reasonable to suppose that there will be healthy one-design racing internationally in a small number of classes: whether these will ultimately be dictated by a committee or whether they will dominate through sheer strength of numbers remains to be seen. Whichever is the case, they will offer a valuable alternative to the present handicap system which favours those owners who can afford to build anew to every small modification of the IOR.

Meanwhile, we have the Level Rating events. A level-racing regatta was organized in the mid-60s for yachts which in those days rated under the Royal Ocean Racing Club's rule at 22ft (6.6m). The main trophy was to be the One Ton Cup.

Needless to say, the competing boats came to be known as One Tonners and as the popularity of this event grew, and new rating levels came into being, Two Tonners, Three-Quarter Tonners, Half Tonners, Quarters and even Eighth or Mini Tonners evolved. In their own level rating competitions, these classes race on level terms, but each is rated under the IOR and may also compete in normal handicap events. The maximum IOR ratings for these level rating, or Ton Cup, classes are:–

Mini Ton

Quarter Ton

Half Ton

Three-Quarter Ton

One Ton

Two Ton

16ft

18ft

21.7ft

24.5ft

27.5ft

32ft

The International Offshore Rule, in common with its predecessors, relies on a formula which takes into account the vital statistics of a yacht: length, beam, depth, draft and sail area are the most important, with various sub-formulae for items which receive a benefit under the rule, such as the drag which is caused by a boat's propeller and her tenderness, which is calculated by carrying out an inclining test.

With the wholesale exploitation of rating rules over the past few decades, such measurement points as length and beam must be very clearly delineated. Length is defined between the two outer girth stations (the circumference of the hull is measured at specific points fore and aft); beam, too, is measured at a carefully prescribed point between the waterline and the maximum beam dimension.

Because factors such as exaggerated beam and freeboard are not generally considered to be speed-producing factors, they have received benefits under the IOR. Similarly, relatively small rigs have been favoured – although there is a generous allowance on subsidiary downwind sails, such as tall-boys, big-boys and bloopers which are set either to balance the spinnaker or to improve the slot effect between spinnaker and mainsail.

With familiarity, designers have been able to play one feature against another until the IOR boat of the late-70s began to look very dinghy-like – and required nearly the same degree of delicate handling to control the headstrong beast. The rulemakers began to worry about the new breed of ULDB, or ultra-light displacement boat, which they had apparently fostered and their fears were redoubled after the 1977 Sydney-Hobart race, in which several of the more lightly constructed competitors came to grief.

The Offshore Rating Council drew up some hasty recommendations and held a meeting in the spring of 1978, with the intention that some quite dramatic changes should be made to the IOR in order to reverse the trend towards very light construction.

But it seems that as fast as they closed one loophole, they opened another. It is ture that the real lightweight flyers' days are numbered, for the results of the spring 1978 meeting will come into force in January 1979, when many boats will find themselves with dramatically increased ratings, hence with no future chance of being competitive against others. However, within a few days of that meeting, radical yacht designers the world over were pointing out new ways to take advantage of the new benefits which the revised rule bestows on certain design features.

Doubtless more rule revisions are in the offing. Meanwhile there would seem to be no reason to anticipate a sudden return to the long, narrow, heavy designs of years gone by.

12 Racing at all levels

Small boat racing

There is something special about a sailboat race, a sense of occasion, a demand for that extra little bit of care in rigging, a tension that has been known to turn a normally calm personality into a jibbering tyrant, unable to keep a crew for more than a single race outing. Those with a competitive spirit, who revel in the ability to think calmly and to maintain peak performance during the course of a race lasting several hours, invariably progress to the top echelons of their chosen fleet. Others, lacking such spirit or self-discipline, derive just as much pleasure from regular competition at local club level – many would say more pleasure, free as it is from the hassle of packing, trailing and travelling to a different venue each weekend.

The local club race will be most people's inauguration into the delights of racing. It will depend on the club whether this is a happy-go-lucky affair on a flooded gravel pit, with the officer of the day bellowing 'no, not yet, Joe . . . your start isn't for another five minutes' through a loud hailer, or whether it is a formal occasion, presided over by gentlemen in white yachting hats, trigger fingers poised over electronic starting equipment and ready to disqualify any skipper with the temerity to cross the starting line early.

It does a skipper no harm to join in a race early on in his sailing career, provided he is confident that he can handle his boat well in all reasonable wind and wave conditions. He is unlikely to shine at first and if he accepts this and keeps well out of the way of the sea lawyers and their tactical battles for supremacy, he will benefit greatly from the discipline which a race imposes. Travelling in the same direction at (more or less) the same speed and at the same time as other boats of the same design is an excellent way to study the vagaries of the wind and the effect of alterations to the boat's trim in certain weather conditions. And there is even more to be learned by discussing the race afterwards

with the other competitors over a refreshing draught.

The next step up the racing ladder is the local regatta, probably within sailing rather than trailing distance, and after that perhaps a week-long championship, provided it is not subject to a limited entry of stars

Learning young: young sailors gather for a Royal Yachting Association-organised race training week at London's Queen Mary Sailing Club.

Launching for a local club race: most sailors' inauguration into
the delights of dinghy racing. *Martin Treadway*

Much more of a spectator sport, even for the novice spectator: a
snarl-up under spinnaker as a large, well-matched fleet rounds a
turning mark. *Yachting World*

The first taste of championship racing can be daunting, but can ensure the travelling bug will bite.

who have previously qualified by their good performances at a series of open meetings.

A week at a championship can kill or cure the racing bug. It can be a superb holiday, interspersed with some excellent competition. It can as easily be a disaster, calling for early starts, a long sail to and from the racing area in adverse weather and at the end of it all an indifferent choice of evening sustenance and entertainment. As much depends on the weather as the venue, and a good host club with good facilities can do a lot to offset any shortcomings on either front.

If the first big regatta or championship is a success, the bug will bite. The circuit of open meetings becomes a must and money which might have been spent on a new bedroom carpet goes instead towards the purchase of a good trailer and a reliable car. But that is not the end of it: every meeting takes its toll of the pocket money on the basics, such as entry fees, petrol and accommodation: these are the outlays which restrict so many potential champions.

Expenses are higher for the keelboat sailor than for the dinghy owner. Everything has to be bigger and stronger and host clubs tend to be those rather professional, hence expensive, ones which boast their own crane facilities. Therefore keelboats tend to remain on their own patch of water and restrict themselves to competitions to which they can sail. Even the widely spread and international classes have fewer fixtures in their racing calendars than their centreboard counterparts, tending to foregather for a series over several weekends at a single venue if a set of qualifying races is prescribed for a big event.

After the area or national championship comes the big international regatta. No racing fanatic should miss the opportunity to attend at least one truly international event. The hustling, bustling, almost circuslike atmosphere and the wealth of ancillary support such as the travelling chandlers and 'pit-men' is seldom reproduced at an indigenous regatta. At first there is a natural reserve in approaching a foreign competitor for advice or just a chat over the day's racing. But that breaks down amazingly fast: there's so much development news to be exchanged, so many notes to compare, even the possibility that a lasting friendship may be struck: one which will help to save on accommodation bills at future overseas events! To some the world

The hustle and bustle of an international regatta dinghy park.
Wendy Fitzpatrick

There are many who say that a world championship, like this one
for 505s in Bermuda, is the epitome of dinghy racing – that the
Olympics are just an expensive joke. Certainly, the standard of
racing tends to be maintained throughout the fleet in such an
event as this, whereas at the Olympics, which allow only one
contestant per country with no minimum qualification, there are
some real rabbits at the tail end. *Alastair Black.*

By the time a skipper reaches Olympic class, he will spend more
time working on his boat than sailing it. *Jack Knights*

championship is the climax of the racing season; but the
big, multi-class international regatta takes a lot of
beating – and usually takes place in a much more
relaxed atmosphere.

Olympic sailing is a very specialized, minority
branch of the sport demanding of much time and
devotion, hence available to only a few. Strangely,
those at the peak of an Olympic class may be faced with
a comparatively small outlay on equipment: manufacturers are often pleased to provide inexpensive goodies
to their chosen stars in exchange for a reliable feed-back
of information on the field-trials. But before a crew can
reach this euphoric state, they must have worked their
way right to the top – and they can do this only through
dedication, hard work, talent and, yes, expenditure of
hard earned cash.

Olympic sailors must be amateurs under a rule of the
International Olympic Committee. To say that every
one fulfils this requirement to the letter may be
stretching the point slightly: an arbitrary ruling that a
sailor may not actually be paid to sail is generally
accepted as the definition of amateur but there is a very
fine dividing line between this, the actual receipt of
sponsorship money and the giving of free time by an
employer so that an employee may devote most of his
talents to an Olympic campaign. And what of the
fortunate minority in some of the world's armed forces
who, exhibiting some talent, are instantly posted to a
'job' which exists only to foster this 'amateur' pursuit of
sport? It is hardly surprising, then, that a great many of
the world's top sailors gravitate towards the marine
industry as a means of earning their daily bread. The
9am-5pm office clerk regards them as true professionals;
the Olympic Committee does not (unless they allow
their names to be used for advertising). Many jobs in
the world of boats are twenty-four hours per day jobs, so
the budding Olympian is able to log much of his
training time to this development programme or that
trial sail for his company should the need arise.

What makes an Olympic sailor? Initially, just a lust
for gold. One specific piece of gold: that round medal
bearing the five Olympic rings.

Soon he becomes enmeshed in the atmosphere of the
Olympic circus. Physically, he must suit one of the six
classes which have Olympic status. Suddenly it becomes second nature to jog every day and visit the
gymnasium two or three times per week because he
knows that physical fitness allows him to stay fresh out
on the course – and that an active brain is not born of a
tired body.

If he is good enough he will probably be asked to join
his country's training squad; training both on and off
the water on most weekends of the year. A training
weekend may start with a Friday night lecture several

hundreds of miles away from home which makes nonsense of a strict working schedule. To remain competitive he must constantly be assessing new masts, sails and equipment and it is as well to have an idea how anything new stands up before launching it straight into a qualifying competition.

So midweek practice is vital, hence a home and a crew close to the water. But it is not all sailing: the ratio of work on the boat ashore to time spent afloat can be as high as 10:1 and when it is considered that that '1' represents more time afloat than the average club sailor's commitment, it will be appreciated that the Olympic God eats, drinks and sleeps boats, sailing and preparation.

Team Racing

A tactical battle – that is, using the racing rules to manoeuvre a fellow competitor into a poor position, will not necessarily win an individual race. It may keep a chosen boat astern and this, at the end of a long series, may be enough to prevent him gaining valuable points which he needs to do well. But the advantage of manoeuvring tactically can quickly be negated by the inevitable slowing in speed of the two (or more) combatants which will give an uninvolved third party the chance to slip ahead.

There is, however, a specialist branch of racing which relies heavily on tactics and a thorough knowledge of the racing rules. Coincidentally, it is often the most interesting type of sailboat racing for the spectator, provided that spectator is *au fait* with the manoeuvres; the casual observer will have a higher regard for a mass of yachts under prettily coloured spinnakers than for a small group of boats seemingly hell-bent on sailing anywhere but in a straight line.

The name of this particular game is team racing. As its name implies it is a race between teams of boats, usually three per side with only two teams racing at once. Individual glory counts for nothing in team racing, the whole object of the race being to prevent the opposition from finishing in a so-called winning combination. The lowest score wins and the scoring is $\frac{3}{4}$-point for a first place, 2 points for second, 3 for third and so on down to sixth. Retirements add 6, disqualifications usually 10 and there is now a system of accepting a $2\frac{1}{2}$ point penalty for an admitted infringement of the rules. Without this, hours can be wasted in hearing unnecessary and acrimonious protests.

Although there is a $\frac{1}{4}$-point bonus for finishing first this does not automatically mean that a three-boat team with a first place will win the match. If numbers two and three can do no better than 5th and 6th (and with the whole of the other side joining forces to deny

This is the sort of configuration the spectator can expect during a team race. Nothing spectacular – but valuable watching, if you know what you're watching for. *Martin Treadway*

them clear wind this is quite possible) the team's score will be $\frac{3}{4}+5+6=11\frac{3}{4}$. The others, meanwhile, have snatched 2nd, 3rd and 4th positions for a score of 9 points. They are, therefore, the victors assuming no penalty points.

Only practice forms a well co-ordinated team. They must be in charge of the match and ready to join forces to lure the opposition back into the fray or sail the opposing side off course in order to allow a team mate through the moment they are threatened. The easy way to calculate whether or not a team is in a winning combination is to look at the race in three groups of two. If a team is leading two of the three pairs (if its positions are 2nd, 3rd and 5th, it is losing the first pair but leading the second and third pairs) it has an overall advantage.

There exist special team racing rules which amplify the basic yacht racing rules to allow such tactics as sailing the opposition 'way off course deliberately, tactics which might in individual competition be the subject of a protest about baulking or unfair sailing.

Match racing: one identical boat against another. Tactics and crew work count for everything. *Ajax News Photos*

Ocean racing: invented by sadists for masochists? *Ajax News Photos*

Match Racing

Match racing is much the same as team racing but with only one pair instead of three; that is, only one boat per side. On a smaller scale, yet on a grander scale, because team races tend to involve dinghies whereas match races are two-boat confrontations and tend to be fought in larger boats. The America's Cup is probably the most famous match race in the world. Certainly it involves the largest yachts.

A good match race is all tactics. It is essential to have the jump on the opposition at every turn – to keep him covered by being on his wind whenever possible. The start is critical: the combatants will manoeuvre and out-manoeuvre each other, sometimes for minutes after the gun has sounded, for the chance to start the race at an advantage.

Ocean Racing

It's three o'clock in the morning when a hoarse and far from seductive voice wakens you from your slumbers. 'Sorry old mate, but you've had your three hours and we're all (expletive deleted) whacked out. Tumble out, will you.' You groan and clutch your pillow only to discover that it is a sodden old sweater. You roll over and fall off the heap of sails – no sleeping allowed in the leeward bunks and your watch mates grabbed the only two windward pipecots. At least you haven't got to take off your pyjamas and change. You are still wearing underclothes, two T shirts, thermal suit, three sweaters, jeans, chest high waterproof trousers, quilt lined heavy nylon ocean racing jacket, safety harness, lifejacket and boots – all soaked right through long since.

Pausing briefly to retie neck towel and jam on cap or sou'wester, you scramble to your feet, only to descend rather more promptly down the 30° diesel-covered chute that purports to be a non-slip cabin sole. Up the ladder and 'clip on' yells a voice from the pitch black horizontal rain and spray-laden atmosphere above decks. 'Wake up laddie and get two reefs in double quick' and you're off again.

Ah, but yesterday! Sun sparkled sea and spanking Force 4 as you bade goodbye to the Isle of Wight and set off south-west under big kite and blooper with a hey-ho for the delights of La Gastronomie Brittanique.

Ocean racing is a sport invented by sadists for the enjoyment of masochists. The subtle twist is that oftimes it is so enjoyable that masochists are frustrated and the sadists get bonus points.

This heavy end of the wide-ranging sailing game is thought by many to be the prerogative of the very rich. To be sure someone foots the considerable bills, but for every crew of nine or ten at least eight are enjoying a unique experience in this generally boring life, for little more than the cost of their special clothing – and for the very best ones, not even that.

Ocean racers vary in size from the minis, some as small as 18ft (5.5m) overall, to the maxi-raters up to about 80ft (24m). Bigger yachts than this race in one-off events such as the Singlehanded trans-Atlantic but most ocean races are restricted to boats which have a maximum IOR rating of 70ft (21m).

Ocean racers of any size are normally distinguishable from their cruising sisters by their Spartan accommodation, taller, more powerful rigs and the com-

It can be more crowded offshore than the subway in the rush hour. Good timing and teamwork are essential. *Alastair Black*

plexity of winches and other deck gear needed to tame that power. To handle the brutes takes teamwork of the highest order and a well drilled crew will all take a predetermined part of the total task in any manoeuvre. When changing sails or rounding marks the 'deck-boss' and his team can win or lose the shorter race or make a difference to a long race result every bit as crucial as the efforts of the man at the helm. A key member of any crew is the navigator and many a good skipper will spend his time navigating and delegate the driving to one or two trustworthy men on each watch.

The keen tyro with small boat experience and sufficient enthusiasm to study navigation is a rare and valuable prize for any boat. Many race short-handed whilst would-be Drakes and Nelsons languish ashore. They have only to join a club with small boats as well as large, sail the former hard until most of their mistakes have been made and then haunt the bar until the right introductions are made to the big boat scene.

Once aboard the ocean racer the novice should be given a comprehensive tour of inspection by the owner, skipper or experienced hand familiar with the boat. High on the priority list is emergency equipment. Items such as liferaft, lifebuoy, marker buoy, flares and the like are required by the racing rules but every boat has different stowage systems and it is vital to be able to locate and use emergency equipment in jig time, even in darkness.

Next will come the chores of preparing for sea. Stowing loose items is not just for tidiness' sake. Safety and efficiency are greatly impaired by mobile mares' nests. Much of the cordage will be stripped off the decks when the boat is at moorings or marina and re-reeving is required before sailing. With several headsails, and special downwind sails – spinnakers, bloopers, big-boys *et al*, – the sidedecks may resemble a cat's cradle and woe betide the man who crosses lines which must lift and which consequently tangle and jam when sails are set.

The beginner can help by clearing up fenders and

Spinnaker trimming offshore: the guy with the tail of the sheet calls the shots to the winch grinder (far right). Notice how the simple rope purchase of the small dinghy has evolved into a powerful hydraulic ram for this offshore racer's boom vang.
Alastair Black

mooring lines and by supplying muscle for sail hoisting as the show goes on the road.

Before starting the race there are duties to be assigned, watches to be picked if the race goes much beyond twelve hours and a great deal of sail packing and preparation for expected conditions of weather and course. The navigator makes bold predictions of tides and weather and experience and memory are called upon to select appropriate sails from the commonly large assortment on board. It is not unknown for a cabin to be so filled with sails that it is impossible to go below without walking on them.

Rules are now in force to limit these absurd arms races but good seamanship and racing interest demand a reasonable variety of choice.

The best organized teams will keep records of rigs used in the different conditions and will create diagrams or tables to aid their fallible memories when attempting to recreate that magic winning set-up.

Whatever complications of rig choice are created by

the weather, the start line and the first leg of the course will also affect sails hoisted and those kept handy for changes or additions. Unlike most small boat races the courses are fixed or possibly confined to one or two alternatives long before the day. The nature of the first leg is then a haphazard affair – just as likely to be a dead run as a beat to windward but on average a reaching start is most common. The keen crews will fight like a dinghy fleet for the favoured end of the line but a great many will opt out of the terrifying milling of the giants – one would be safer ballet dancing with a herd of elephants.

The start will be further enlivened if spinnakers are to be hoisted at the gun – it is easy to appreciate why ocean racers accept a time penalty for being over the line, when a dinghy in the same situation would be expected to return and restart.

The start, then, is a time for all hands on deck and the best man available steering. Soon after this melee, however, the action settles down to the deliberate pace

When the offshore skipper says 'frog', you jump. *Alastair Black*

of the long distance race of any sport. With a mixture of rig sizes and boat speeds the smaller competitors with good starts will arc up to windward to let the tardy heavy mob pass without blanketing their wind. Such small deviations are not significant on a leg several miles long and the fleet will spread over a much larger area than would be the case in shorter races.

Another reason for widely diverging courses will be the different navigators' estimates of tidal effects. Certain marks of the course or coastal headlands will create 'tidal gates'. The gate is an area through which all must pass but at certain times the foul tidal stream may be so powerful that it is impossible to make any headway against it. The navigator has the thankless task of estimating whether his yacht can make a gate during its 'open' time, that is, when the tidal stream is either slack or favourable, by taking a risk of crossing deep water. If he is wrong, the boat may be swept back with little chance of anchoring whilst the more conservative opposition gain by creeping round the coast.

Judgments must also be made on likely changes in the weather. Success goes to those with a combination of knowledge and boldness.

As the hours tick by the fleet will disperse so widely that many a competitor will have only one or two others in sight, perhaps none at all. The temptation to relax is always present but the potential winners will always act as if their opposition is just ahead of them.

When a watchkeeping system is ordained, the experienced hand will take his kip come tempest, storm or noonday sun. He remembers only too well the cameo at the start of this section. This old salt will also know the value of sea-sickness pills – it is not clever to stand up to it all day and collapse just when you are needed – and he will eat regularly and lightly of high energy foods.

Thus fortified and rested he will be bright-eyed and bushy tailed, changing sails and fighting hard all the way to the finish line, ready to collect the happy silverware and enjoy the run ashore.

Be warned, though, the sadist is still present and the unrepentant masochist has been forced to grin and bear the sad news that 'the tide is down and we can't get over the bar at the harbour mouth for another 6 hours. There's a storm brewing and we can't lie on a lee shore. Reef her down, turn her round and make ready for another wet night in mid-Channel.'

13 Some classic races

It is difficult to pinpoint the factors which turn a yacht race into a classic yacht race. It is not necessarily the size of the fleet, the distance they sail, the size of the boats involved or the seniority of the event itself. It is not even the cost of preparing a yacht for entry. Every country has its own, be it a carefree day race like the UK's Round the Isle of Wight Race or a serious thrash like Canada's West Coast Swiftsure Classic. There is a handful of ocean racing crews who do nothing but travel the world offshore circuit.

America's Cup

Few events command such a depth of involvement from such a wealth of talent as the two-boat, best of seven race series which is the America's Cup. In 1851 the 101ft (30m) schooner 'America' sailed across to England shortly after her launch and proved to the British yachting world how far they lagged behind their trans-Atlantic cousins in the realms of both design and rig. Having outpaced everything that floated in the Channel, 'America' lined up with a small fleet of British yachts, ranging from 40-300 tons (40-300 tonnes), for a race around the Isle of Wight for which the Royal Yacht Squadron had put up a trophy, the One Hundred Guinea Cup.

The vastly superior windward performance of 'America', coupled with a chapter of disasters which befell the faster boats among the British fleet, gave the big schooner a runaway victory and brought the now legendary exchange on shore. Queen Victoria, upon enquiring which yachts had crossed the line first and second, received the reply " 'America', your Majesty, there is no second".

The first commodore of the New York Yacht Club, Commodore Stevens, was at the helm of 'America' during her visit to England and it was the Commodore, together with the syndicate which had had 'America' built to a George Steers design, who presented the One Hundred Guinea Cup (also known quite erroneously as the Queen's Cup, for Queen Victoria had no involvement with it) to the New York Yacht Club as an international challenge trophy under these conditions:–

'Any organised yacht club of any foreign country shall always be entitled, through any one or more of its members, to claim the right of sailing a match for this Cup with any yacht or vessel of not less than 30 tons (30.483 tonnes) or more than 300 tons (304.83 tonnes). The parties desiring to sail for the Cup may make any match with the yacht club in possession of the same that may be determined upon by mutual consent: but in case of disagreement as to terms, the match shall be sailed over the usual course for the annual regatta of the yacht club in possession of the Cup, and subject to its rules and sailing regulations – the challenging party being bound to give six months' notice in writing, fixing the day they wish to start.'

By now the cup had come to be known as the America's Cup after the schooner which won it and it was laid down in the conditions of the challenge that it should never become the property of an owner, but of the yacht club through which the owner challenged.

It was not until 1870 that the first challenge was received, from James Ashbury of England in his deep-draught schooner 'Cambria'. She, like 'America', had to compete against a veritable fleet of defenders including many centreboarders which were highly developed, specialized craft capable of a good turn of speed and ideally suited to the shoal waters off the Eastern Seaboard. It was hardly fair, said the English, that a boat which had had to sail across the Atlantic on her own bottom should have to face this sort of opposition.

But even when the size of the defending fleet was reduced to one for his next challenge in 1871, Ashbury – this time challenging with a relatively over-canvassed schooner called 'Livonia' – felt himself still to be at a

Sir Thomas Lipton's 'Shamrock V', the last of an era, was the UK challenger for the America's Cup in 1931. *Central Press Photos Ltd*

o' mutton rig and gaff rigged racing yachts began to be a thing of the past.

But the J Class, too, were doomed. Traditionally linked with the America's Cup and seemingly for such a long period, the magnificent Js in fact raced in only three challenges, Sir Thomas Lipton's final challenge with 'Shamrock V' against 'Enterprise' and Sir Thomas Sopwith's two pre-war challenges with his 'Endeavours' against 'Rainbow' and 'Ranger' respectively.

The Js fell victim of the Second World War and even their successors in America's Cup racing, the smaller Twelve Metres, were of such a size as to be an impossible extravagance in the immediate post-war years. The challenge was not renewed until the late 50s, but has gained momentum steadily since then, with a refreshing variety of countries showing a tangible interest: Australia, France and Sweden, where previously only two Canadian challenges had broken the run of fourteen from the UK.

During the 70s so many challenges were received that the challengers were obliged to hold their own elimination trials to select the country which would face the defender.

But still the Cup, known affectionately as the Auld Mug, rests in the New York Yacht Club. Perhaps the 1980 challenge will succeed where others have failed. For the first time there is reason to hope that those European countries which covet the Cup will come together to race their Twelve Metres as a fleet, to provide a yardstick for the boat which eventually wins the right to challenge after elimination trials between the four challenging countries.

Other match races

The America's Cup has always tested design and rig as much as racing talent, as does the smaller Canada's Cup, held on the Great Lakes since the end of the 1800s. So, in a very different way, does the International Catamaran Challenge Trophy which was once dubbed the 'Little America's Cup' by a UK yachting journalist, and is now known more by its nickname than its correct title. The Catamaran Challenge series is for the giant C Class cats and victory has been spread between the UK, Australia, the USA and even Denmark. Momentum was lost in the UK when its C Class Catamaran Association seemed to run out of funds and enthusiasm when defeat followed a long run of successes by the famous 'Lady Helmsman'. It appears to have faded in the US, too, where Tony de Mauro of Rowayton is one of the few remaining enthusiasts. His 'Patient Lady III' beat the 1977 challenge from the Australian 'Nicholas II' to retain the trophy.

Match racing must be more suited to boats which are

disadvantage, for the American hosts reserved the right to field a different defender for each race if they felt like it.

This challenge was the first, but unfortunately not the last, to be dogged by a considerable amount of acrimony; perhaps the worst being the so-called 'Dunraven Affair' during the English Earl of Dunraven's second challenge in 1895 with 'Valkyrie III'. The Earl proved himself a less than perfect sportsman after a series of incidents had just not gone his way.

Fortunately Sir Thomas Lipton came along in the 20s and 30s to heal any breach of trans-Atlantic *bonhomie*. His was not only a good natured series of challenges but also marked the beginning of an era. With the adoption on both sides of the Atlantic of Lloyd's Register of Shipping's scantlings rules for yachts built under their survey, also of the J Class rule, the mammoth schooners and cutters faded from the America's Cup matches. In the 20s, too, great strides were made sin the development on the bermudan, or leg known to be evenly matched and in this lies the strength of the Congressional Cup – and the newer series of the same name raced off Lymington in the UK. Stock cruiser/racers – Cal 40s, Contessa 32s – are used for the series to which leading helmsmen are invited, each racing individually against the rest to determine the overall winner.

Cowes Week

The Isle of Wight lies just a few miles (kilometres) south of the south coast of England, more or less opposite the long estuary of the rivers Test, Itchen and Hamble which surround the busy port of Southampton. The River Medina flows from the island at its northernmost point and it is on the mouth of this river that Cowes lies.

It is an unlikely yachting centre, opening as it does on-to the busy commercial Solent (the stretch of water which separates the island and the mainland) with its sluicing double tides. But it has grown up as the fashionable resort of a fashionable sport and today it is traditionally regarded as the mecca of British yachting.

One of the problems of Cowes: with an adverse tidal stream and a short first leg, most of the fleet can arrive at the first mark simultaneously. This is Class 5 for boats of about Quarter Ton size. *Studio 77*

'Lady Helmsman', several times defender of the International Catamaran Challenge, in her heyday. This wing mast is quite conventional by modern day standards: the size, weight and expense of devloping these rigs is one reason for the C-Cat's decline in popularity. *Studio 77*

Many yachtsmen based at equally 'yachty' venues around the UK would disagree violently but arguments that conditions off Cowes are unsuitable for fair competition have been countered by the argument that it is the obstacles to fair competition, such as those found on a championship golf course, which separates the true champion from The Rest.

There has been a regatta at Cowes for as long as the Royal Yacht Squadron has existed. Cowes Week as it is known today has been held since the 30s, always placed strategically in the social calendar between Goodwood and the opening of the grouse season. To the chagrin of some yacht owners, the Glorious Twelfth (12th August, when grouse shooting becomes legal in the UK) actually clashes with the final racing of Cowes Week in some years because it is truthfully Goodwood, which always commences on the final Tuesday of July, which dictates the Cowes Week schedule.

The Week is now held over nine days, from Saturday to Sunday inclusive, but before the war racing on Sundays was taboo – it was Sir Ralph Gore who was instrumental in overcoming the ban on Sunday racing, citing as his precedent the wont of polo followers to play on Sundays. The Royal Yacht Squadron now mans the starter's platform on three of those days, handing over its starting line to race committees of neighbouring Cowes and mainland clubs on the remaining six.

Cowes Week is an institution. Local hotel owners add a barely believable premium to their charges during the Week, but this is all part of the ambience and it is this, not necessarily the racing, which brings the regulars back year after year. Back to the overcrowded marinas; the unwieldy, swaying trots; the launches ferrying anyone from a butcher's boy to a prince hither and thither across the Medina; the constant nightmare of the ferry, hydrofoil and hovercraft pilots trying to enter the narrow channel against an armada of competitors swarming, lemming-like, to their start; the pleading and cajoling and parting with vast quantities of cash in order to be the proud possessor of a badge which entitles the wearer to pass into the local yacht clubs; the *bonhomie* of those who did not bother with such niceties as they foregather in the temporary marina bar or around the equally temporary hamburger bus. At six o'clock in the evening barefoot boat crews pass dinner-jacketed flag officers in the High Street. At six o'clock in the morning, well lubricated Jack Tars are still searching in vain for the liberty boat which took their mates back to their ship some hours earlier. One yacht's crew went as far as to turn out for the day's racing in full evening attire on the morning after the Cowes Week Ball.

It takes nearly three hours to start all the Cowes Week classes at ten minute intervals, the largest ocean racers going away around 10am, the last of the local small keelboat classes not racing until after 1pm.

Round the Island Race

If there is a degree of frivolity in the attitude of some crews towards Cowes Week racing, there is a near-total lack of dedication to winning Britain's largest yacht race. Over four hundred boats of all shapes and sizes enter the annual Round the Island Race which starts at an unearthly hour in the morning from Cowes and returns there later in the day – or when the tides deem fit. This truly is a family jamboree; the time to take the kids and the dog for a jaunt around the Isle of Wight in company with others. Small wonder, then, that the hot-shot racers who take it seriously usually sweep the silverware.

Fastnet Race

Britain's Royal Ocean Racing Club inaugurated a new offshore race in 1925, over an often rugged 605-mile (973km) course around the Fastnet Rock off the Irish Coast. The Fastnet is now run biennially, starting, in the years that it is held, on the final Friday of Cowes Week.

Winner of the first Fastnet was a Le Havre pilot cutter called 'Jolie Brise', an all-gaff-and-bowsprit charmer whose success in this admittedly limited fleet only served to enhance the opinion of traditionalists that proven working boats had the edge on pure racing yachts over a long sea course. 'Jolie Brise' made a guest appearance in the 70s to celebrate the twenty-fifth Fastnet Race but the old lady fell victim of the fogs and calms which dogged the event and she retired to Cowes.

What a contrast was the winner just six years later, the Olin Stephens-designed yawl 'Dorade', slim and racy and in the Metre boat tradition. 'Dorade' was the easy winner of a trans-Atlantic feeder race from Newport to Plymouth in a time of only seventeen days.

Admiral's Cup

It was to boost international interest in its Fastnet Race that the Royal Ocean Racing Club, in conjunction with the Royal Yacht Squadron, inaugurated the Admiral's Cup in 1957. It can hardly be claimed to have been a roaring success in those early days, the home team beating off a solitary challenge from the USA and repeating its success in 1959 against a two-pronged attack from France and Germany.

The cup went overseas for the first time in 1961, to the USA, and then returned to British shores for two series before falling into Australian hands in 1967 –

The Portuguese sail training ship 'Sagres'. Very few countries can afford such immense training
ships, but we are grateful to those which can for giving us a glimpse of the seascape of yesteryear.
John Watney

The wind is only light, but Germany's 'Rubin' is trickling along nicely under a cloud of canvas.
John Watney

The epitome of Cowes Week. Dragons, the ex-Olympic three-man keelboat, are one of the thirteen inshore classes. The leaders of this race are just passing the famed Green, close-hauled for the finishing line off the Royal Yacht Squadron. *John Watney*

Ocean Racers, like thoroughbred horses, turn up in many guises. The successful Bob Miller-designed Australian 'Ginkgo' reappeared the following year as 'Guia' in the Italian Admiral's Cup team. *John Watney*

perhaps predictably, for the Aussies, having come a close second in the previous series with three old boats, had gone to town on their second attempt and built anew . . . but even so the oldest of the original trio, the slim 'Caprice of Huon', had proved herself so suited to British waters that she returned to the fray. The USA, Britain and Germany have been the winners in recent years, but never by a runaway margin.

Admiral's Cup competition from twenty countries is now the norm, the vast majority building for the series specially designed boats to suit the anticipated conditions. It is always a gamble, for the only predictable thing about the British weather is its sheer unpredictability. A high over the Azores can bring a fortnight of balmy breezes or can as easily give way to a period of stormy weather. The once traditional Solent sou'wester may fizzle to a calm as a seabreeze is prevented from reaching the Solent by the mass of the Island itself. A 'small' boat—the AC range is between about 35ft and 55ft (35m—16.5m) overall—which is reckoned to be favoured for the relatively light conditions of the inshore races can, for example, turn into an embarrassment for her team if bad weather is encountered during the Fastnet.

The series now comprises three inshore races of about 30 miles (48km), carrying single points; one medium-length offshore race, the Channel Race of about 225 miles (362km) which carries double points; and the Fastnet Race which carries a triple points bonus. The adage that a race is never over until it is won was never more true than when describing the Admiral's Cup series. A good performance in the Fastnet Race, coming as it does at the end of the series, can pluck a team out of the doldrums and on to the winner's podium.

SORC and the Southern Cross

The UK has its Fastnet, the US has had the Newport to

Classic backdrop of Table Mountain for the start of the Cape-Rio Race, now renamed the South Atlantic Race and scheduled to arrive in Uruguay, not Rio, for political reasons. *Central Press Photos Ltd*

Bermuda Race since 1906; in Australia the classic is the Sydney-Hobart. Australia picked up her cue from the UK and introduced the Southern Cross series, an event along the lines of the Admiral's Cup but less often frequented by European teams because of the expense of transportation. Like the AC, the Southern Cross culminates in a classic long-distance race: the Sydney to Hobart, which traditionally starts on Boxing Day and almost as traditionally is over a course favouring boats which can handle a long, spanking downwind leg followed by a slog to windward across the Bass Strait and into Hobart. These are the conditions to which Australian offshore thinking is geared, which makes the country's success over the flatter water of the Admiral's Cup courses so meritworthy.

The USA's SORC – Southern Ocean Racing Conference to give it its full title, or Southern Circuit for short – takes some beating for a test of boat and crew. The seemingly idyllic waters off Florida and the Bahama Islands can be anything but idyllic and this series of long offshore races often takes a heavy toll of gear.

One hundred or so boats compete in at least part of the series, but usually little more than half see it through to the bitter end – most being unable or unwilling to spare the time needed: just about the whole of February and a little bit of March.

The races include a 140-mile (225km) from St Petersburg to Boca Grande and back, a 400-mile (643km) from St. Petersburg to Miami via a circuitous route, a near-200 mile (321km) ocean triangle off Florida followed by a slightly shorter one before the 200-mile Miami-Nassau race and, finally a round the buoys race off Nassau.

Cape-Rio Race

Why, thought a group of South Africans in 1970, should other countries have their very own long distance races, but not SA? Cape Town seemed a good place to start, but the coasts of the continent were on the inhospitable side and potential finishing ports either inadequate or politically unstable.

Nothing daunted and several sundowners to the good, an action committee was formed to plan the boldest ocean race yet – a three thousand mile dash to Rio de Janiero, arriving in that cosmopolitan port to coincide with its famed carnival.

In 1971 their dreams came true and a fleet of 58 took up the challenge. By the third race in 1975 the fleet was nearly 130: the race was on the map.

Unfortunately, politics reared an ugly head and future races will be redirected to Uruguay, the race to be known as the South Atlantic Race.

Round the World Race

It had to happen. After the inauguration of the Golden Globe award for the first man to sail around the world alone, there just had to be an all-out race for fully crewed yachts. The idea had its detractors, of course, those who were convinced that tragedy would be heaped upon tragedy and indeed they were right, for three crew members lost their lives on the very first race. There was happily no such disaster on the second.

But the anti lobby did not triumph over the tremendous depth of enthusiasm for this longest ocean race of all time. Promoters of other classics were beginning to run out of superlatives when this one came along but now there can be no longer ocean race until man lands on a larger water-covered planet than Earth.

It is said that one Round the World Race is equal to between eleven and fifteen years of normal ocean racing – and if you think it's a hard slog for the crews of those ocean giants, just imagine how much more discomfort can be inflicted on the crews of the smaller fry. Take the Polish 'Copernicus', for example, at 45ft (13.5m), the smallest boat in that first race, whose five-man crew sailed her every inch of the way. Compare that with the British 'Adventure' and 'British Soldier' which changed their crews of ten at every port of call. Interestingly the two Brits finished second and ninth overall. And 'Copernicus'? Eleventh.

In 1969 two British publishers, Anthony Churchill and Guy Pearse, mooted the idea of a fully crewed yacht race round the world. By 1972 the enthusiastic reception of their idea had evolved into firm entries from responsible owners and organizations in several countries. There remained only one obstacle: finance.

By now the Royal Naval Sailing Association was nearly totally committed to the venture as a crew training exercise, if nothing else. Moreover, the Association reckoned it could find the necessary backing to enable the race to go ahead. And so, in the spring of '72 the preliminary work was handed over to the RNSA and the brewers, Whitbread, moved in to provide the necessary financial support. D-Day was set for 8th

The crew of 'Heath's Condor' chewed their way through this and more on the Round the World Race. *Yachts & Yachting*

September 1973, the race to take about eight months, the course to be:–

'From Portsmouth to Cape Town, Sydney, thence via Cape Horn to Rio de Janiero and back to Portsmouth. The race will be stopped and re-started at Cape Town, Sydney and Rio de Janiero.'

Competing yachts would race under the International Offshore Rule and would carry a minimum crew of five. Emergency stops were to be allowed on any convenient area of dry land and sick crew members could be left ashore – but replacements were allowed to be shipped aboard only at the three specified ports of call.

Mindful of the terrors of the open sea, the organizers reiterated in their conditions of entry the ubiquitous disclaimer that the decision to start or continue with a race is the sole responsibility of each competitor, adding two more clauses just to underline the seriousness with which they were undertaking the venture:–

'The safety of a yacht and her crew is the sole and inescapable responsibility of the owner, who must do his best to ensure that the yacht is fully found, thoroughly seaworthy and manned by an experienced crew who are physically fit to face bad weather. He must be satisfied as to the soundness of hull, spars, rigging, sails and all gear. He must ensure that all safety equipment is properly maintained and stowed and that the crew know where it is kept and how it is to be used.'

'Neither the establishment of these special regulations, nor the inspection of a yacht under these regulations in any way limits or reduces the complete and unlimited responsibility of the owner.'

The first race in 1973/4 attracted 20 entries; the second, in 1977/78 seventeen. Both were won by privately-owned yachts in an event which has become predominantly sponsored. The first went to Ramon Carlin's Swan 65 'Sayula' from Brazil; the second to another 65-footer (19.5m), this one a Sparkman & Stephens one-off called 'Flyer', owned by Cornelius von Rietshoten of Holland.

OSTAR

The Observer Singlehanded trans-Atlantic Race is, according to Eric Tabarly in his preface to *Alone*, Daniel Gilles' book of the race, 'the only race of its kind of any real significance'. Tabarly, the adventurous Frenchman, will undoubtedly be disappointed with the organizers' decision to restrict the fleet size for the 1980 race to 110, and the size of the competing boats to 56ft (16.8m)—46ft (13.8m) on the waterline—for he continues '. . . it has been run with virtually no rules or regulations, leaving competitors completely free in their choice of boat, rig and course. To compete you

The two French giants at the start of the 1976 OSTAR, The 4-masted 'Club Mediterranee' and the smaller, but still enormous, 'Vendredi 13'. *Alastair Black*

must, on the one hand, have a wide experience of the sea and of sailing so as to select your own craft, and on the other the qualities of seamanship, navigation and competitive spirit needed to take you over the finishing line in the shortest possible time.'

Colonel 'Blondie' Hasler is the father of the Singlehanded trans-Atlantic Race as we know it. War hero Hasler first suggested such a race to the Slocum Society in New York in the mid-Fifties but they, like so many individuals and organizations after them, seemed worried that encouraging yachtsmen to race so far singlehanded might be considered to be irresponsible. But Hasler persisted and obtained the support of the Royal Western Yacht Club of England, then of the Slocum Society and later the financial backing from the Observer newspaper.

But still there were obstructions from those who feared for the safety of competitors and of shipping in the busy Western Approaches to the English Channel – the English Parliament was high on the list of worried outsiders, until feeling began to run so high that Francis Chichester (he had yet to be knighted) and Blondie Hasler agreed to sail the course for a private wager of just 2/6d (12½p).

However, very little can keep a good idea down once it has received the support of the enthusiasts. The OSTAR was just such an idea and plans began to be made for the first race in 1960.

The course was to be from Plymouth, handily placed on England's South-West coast, to New York. For later races the finishing port was to be changed to Newport, Rhode Island, home of the America's Cup and proud possessor of that yachting metropolis Narragansett Bay. The east to west course on the face of it would be straight into the teeth of the prevailing westerly winds, not to mention through the path of ice floes and fogs in the later stages of the voyage. Icebergs can pose a real threat, for the iceberg zone extends as far south as latitude 40° – more or less level with both the Azores and Newport, although they never reach the eastern part of the Atlantic – and isolated bergs have been recorded as far south as Bermuda. The closing stages of the race, when exhausted singlehanded helmsmen are battling through the frequent fogs and among the busy fishing and commercial traffic off the Newfoundland coast, can be a tremendous strain.

The Great Circle Route, that is, the direct, shortest route between the start and finish is a little short of 3,000 miles (4820km) but it need not necessarily be the fastest route, for the prevailing winds are westerlies – dead-nosers – and often gale force into the bargain.

The northern route, pioneered by Colonel Hasler, is longer but offers the gamble of picking up favourable easterly winds and the certainty of hitching a lift on the favourable Labrador current sooner.

The two southern routes, beloved of competitors with fast multihulls, are appreciably longer, the southern-most which seeks the trade winds south of the Azores and Bermuda over 4,000 miles (6436km) and perhaps the most extreme gamble of all. Statistics would suggest that it pays to sail as close as possible to the Great Circle Route, risking headwinds and gales and taking advantage of all the meteorological data available to plan a tactical, middle-of-the-road course.

One can only guess at the number – and size – of entries the 1980 race would have fielded had no upper limits been imposed by the organisers. From a gallant quintet in that first race in 1960 racing on a first home wins basis, the race has grown rapidly. Fourteen started in 1964, including the original five skippers plus the then little-known Frenchman Eric Tabarly whose name was to become synonymous with special marathon monster craft and whose enthusiasm for the race must have precipitated modern French fanaticism for these events. That was the year, too, that a handicapping system was initiated – although line honours have always been the goal of the publicity conscious; the achievement which has captured the imagination of press and public . . . and sponsor.

1968 brought the organizers' insistence that competing boats complete a qualifying cruise: nineteen finished the race, sixteen retired. The fleet swelled to 55 in 1972, the year when the huge 'Vendredi Treize' dwarfed boats which previously had been considered large at 60 and 70ft (18 and 21m) and which, at a mere 128ft (39m) was in her turn to be dwarfed by the

And this is what 'Club Med' would look like from the deck of a middle-size OSTAR competitor. Not worth arguing with! *Alastair Black*

immense 236ft (72m) 'Club Mediterranée' of Alain Colas in the 1976 race which followed. Her size, and the fact that Colas had nearly severed his foot in a mooring accident and was still convalescing as his entry was made, prompted the race committee to place special requirements on 'Club Med'. Her qualifying cruise of 500 miles (800km) was allowed to be with a full crew; on the other hand Colas himself was required to prove the practicability of the boat as a singlehander by completing an additional 1,500 miles (2400km) on his own. Note that until then finishers in previous races were themselves exempted from personal qualification.

Despite her size, 'Club Med' failed to beat Tabarly's 'Pen Duick' across the line and could finish only third on corrected time to Tabarly's first in class. By now, three classes had been established: the Jester Trophy named after the boat in which the race's founder had taken part for smaller fry of 38ft (11.5m) and under-waterline length 28ft (8.5m); the Gipsy Moth Trophy, named after Sir Francis Chichester's successful 'Gipsy Moth III' for boats with a waterline length between 28ft (8.5m) and 46ft (13.8m) and the Pen Duick Trophy for boats with a waterline length over 46ft.

Sir Francis Chichester, then un-knighted, in the 39ft (11.8m) traditional long-keel wooden sloop 'Gipsy Moth III' was the winner of the first race in 40 days, 12 hours, 30 minutes. He was beaten by nearly three days in the second race by Eric Tabarly in the purpose-designed 44ft (13.4m) ketch 'Pen Duick II' with a time of 27 days, 23 hours—the extra 100 miles (160km) or so which was required to take the competitors to the original New York finishing line accounts for most of this time difference. In 1968, despite his attempt to go even faster in a 67ft (20.4m) trimaran, Tabarly's plans were thwarted by a collision early in the race. A return for hasty repairs was to no avail and he withdrew, leaving the field clear for Geoffrey Williams in the 56ft (17m) ketch 'Sir Thomas Lipton' to clock up 25 days, 20 hours, 33 minutes.

The name 'Pen Duick' came to the fore again in 1972; this was 'PD IV', the 67ft (20.4m) tri (the first multihull to win the OSTAR) with, not Tabarly, but fellow-countryman Alain Colas at the helm. Her time was 20 days, 13 hours, 15 minutes, less than one day ahead of Jean-Yves Terlain's 'Vendredi Treize'.

. . . And yet again in 1976, this time with Tabarly driving to his second victory. This 'Pen Duick' was 'PD VI' which returned to the conventional, if conventional is quite the word for the 73ft (22.2m) aluminium ketch with spent uranium keel which was the product of so much money and attention.

There are other single- and short-handed races: the two-man Round Britain Race and the peculiarly Gallic one-man-and-a-girl race in warmer climes, but none seem to attract quite the same charisma as the OSTAR. The Round Britain, incidentally, was said to be the end of more than one close friendship. It may be better not to enquire too deeply into how relationships fared in the other-mentioned two-handed race.

14 They made a name for themselves

There's no saying what turns a sailor into a marathon voyager. Some, like the Hiscocks, just voyage far and wide in a well-found boat because they love to see the world – the Hiscocks have now circled the world five times in their successive 'Wanderers' and, though Eric Hiscock writes a book of each of his journeys, they seek no glory from their achievement, simply a sense of self-satisfaction at having sailed somewhere new and made new friends.

Others are more individual: David Lewis, for example, who voyages among the icebergs and suffers the misery that only intense cold can bring – again and again, because he loves the polar regions.

Others again are stuntmen: the Evel Knievels of the sailing world. Chay Blyth, the Paratroop sergeant whose fanaticism for adventure training eventually led him to pit himself against the elements by sailing round the world the 'wrong way', against most of the prevailing winds . . . Alain Colas, the Frenchman who drove the 67ft (20.4m) trimaran 'Pen Duick IV' (later 'Manuréva') in the wake of the Clipper Race, just to prove that multihulls really could cope with Cape Horn, the Roaring Forties and the mountainous seas of the Southern Ocean. The Clipper Race, not a resoundingly popular event, was held two years after the first Round the World Race, specifically to attract attempts by modern ocean racing yachts to beat the record of the fastest wool clipper ship of all, 'Patriarch', on the London to Sydney run.

But Colas was not the first to girdle the world in a multihull. Colin and Rosie Swale had already completed a circumnavigation in their production cruising catamaran 'Anneleise', a stunt maybe, but a fine achievement for a young couple who knew little about seamanship when they set out. On their shakedown cruise, Colin was to deliver their first baby with the scant help of a single page of advice in Reed's Nautical Almanac.

For every sailor whose exploits reach the public eye,

there must be fifty who could boast similar achievements but don't: ordinary club sailors who invest all their savings in a boat of their dreams and go off to see at least a part of the world – asking nothing in return save a few pints of liquid refreshment in exchange for showing fellow club members their film of the voyage.

And of those who do hit the headlines, only a minority continue with similar newsworthy exploits. Others, having achieved (or, sadly, failed to achieve) what they set out to achieve, retire to the local creek or even, one suspects, follow the time-honoured adage of shouldering their oars and walking inland until they meet someone who asks what they are carrying . . . and there building their house.

Through the accounts of his voyages, Joshua Slocum has come to be regarded as the father of modern ocean voyaging. Slocum, born in Novia Scotia in the mid 1800s, made the first recorded singlehanded circumnavigation of the world in his 37ft (11.2m) 'Spray', in which he left Boston in April 1895. Journeying via Gibraltar, South Africa, then Cape Horn, the Pacific Ocean, around the east and north coasts of Australia and back to Boston via the Cape of Good Hope and the West Indies, Slocum took a little over three years for the journey in a boat without the latterday luxury of self-steering and which, in his own words, leaked 'not one drop'. Slocum, in his book 'Sailing Around the World', leaves us in no doubt that he sailed on because he wanted to see the world and because he was confident that such a journey was quite within the capabilities of himself and his 'Spray':–

'If the 'Spray' discovered no continents on her voyage, it may be there were no more continents to be discovered. She did not seek new worlds, nor to sail to pow wow about the dangers of the seas. The sea has been much maligned. To find one's way to lands already discovered is a good thing, and the 'Spray' made the discovery that even the worst sea is not so terrible to a well appointed ship.'

Sir Francis Chichester in the cockpit of 'Gypsy Moth IV' in which he sailed round the world singlehanded in 1966/67. *Eileen Ramsay*

Slocum was in no hurry to beat the clock but the same cannot be said of one of the more famous twentieth century adventurers, Sir Francis Chichester. Chichester, as early as 1929, flew solo from London to Sydney in his Gipsy Moth plane and having achieved this set out to fly round the world. The absence of landing strips made it necessary to convert the plane to a seaplane but his attempt was thwarted, for he hit an overhead cable and was brought down into Katsuura harbour. As he grew older, he switched his allegiance to boats, taking 'Gipsy Moth III' in two Singlehanded trans-Atlantic races before commissioning Captain John Illingworth to design him a fast globe-girdler. He wanted to beat the clippers' time of 117 days to Sydney, but this record was not to fall for another decade when both 'Great Britain II' and 'Kriter II' beat the magical figure in 1976.

Chichester was not entirely happy with his 54ft (16.4m) 'Gipsy Moth IV' and, hearing his criticisms,

one is left with the impression that he felt she was just a little too large for one man to handle in all weathers. He had some quite extensive modifications carried out in Australia, before making his way back to England via Cape Horn. The Horn, quite simply, terrified him, he admitted. Yet he researched the disasters which had befallen those who had navigated the route previously and satisfied himself that all were attributable to some inadequacy of boat or crew. There were to be no such inadequacies in the voyage of this remarkable man – who celebrated his sixty-fifth birthday en route.

It was a very frail man at the helm of 'Gipsy Moth IV' at the start of the 1972 trans-Atlantic Race even the routine shiphandling tasks seemed to demand a superhuman effort by Sir Francis Chichester.

Eleven days after the start of the race he was sighted heading for England under reduced sail. Shortly after the sighting Sir Francis radioed that he was weak and requested his son Giles to meet him at Brest.

A French weather ship went to his aid but came too close and damaged 'Gipsy Moth's' rigging. Chichester despatched her and awaited the arrival of his son aboard a Royal Navy frigate. Tragically, the French ship was to meet an American cruising yacht whose crew had also picked up Chichester's message and were sailing into the area to stand by. The collision resulted in loss of life as the cruiser sank.

Sir Francis Chichester, his son Giles and Lieutenant Commander Peter Martin of the Royal Navy sailed 'Gipsy Moth' back to Plymouth, where Chichester was taken to the Naval Hospital. He died there on 25th August 1972.

Mention should be made here of Captain Illingworth, the man who designed Chichester's 'Gipsy Moth IV' and the new rig for Sir Alec Rose's 'Lively Lady'. Illingworth worked as enthusiastically as anyone to promote ocean racing in the pre- and immediately post-war years. Stationed around the world in the Royal Navy he infected others with his enthusiasm wherever he went. In 1946, while in Australia, he was instrumental in persuading the Cruising Yacht Club in Sydney to promote its Christmas cruise to Hobart to race status. The committee agreed and Illingworth entered his 35ft (10.5m) cutter 'Rani', pressing on in a gale of wind which sent other, larger boats scuttling for shelter. The swashbuckling style in which he won this race matches perfectly the press-on-come-hell-or-high-water style for which today's Australian sailors are renowned. Returning to England, Illingworth campaigned 'Maid of Malham', a conventional ocean racer with a then-unconventional masthead rig, and later 'Myth of Malham' whose high freeboard was avant garde but well favoured under the RORC rule of the day. 'Myth' was a remarkably successful boat in the 50s and 60s – she even finished 8th in the OSTAR in 1968 in the hands of Noel Bevan – but she met an ignominious fate when she foundered in the English Channel.

The name of Alec Rose is often uttered in the same breath as that of Chichester, for Rose completed his solo circumnavigation at much the same time and at much the same stage of life. Of the two, Rose is the more homely character: a florist and fruiterer, rather than an adventurer, who took up sailing seriously when his first marriage broke up after nearly thirty years. He and his second wife Dorothy cruised extensively in a lifeboat which he converted himself, until he bought the heavy-displacement 36ft (10.9m) 'Lively Lady' for the 1964 trans-Atlantic Race.

The germ of an idea for sailing round the world was already forming in Rose's mind when Chichester announced his plans. That decided him; he would take the same route at much the same time, though he knew that his 'Lady' would be no match for the bigger, faster, purpose-built 'Gipsy Moth', and he would take the opportunity to visit his son in Australia before leaving to beat the storm season at Cape Horn.

Being slower, Rose needed to leave several weeks before Chichester, in order to meet his schedule and, as planned, he set off early in April 1966. But it was a hasty departure: 'Lively Lady' had not been prepared for sea in the way he would have liked and her main engine would not start, should it have been needed to charge the batteries. 'Never,' he said 'have I started with the ship in such a muddle and so unprepared.' Sure enough, things went from bad to worse and he put into Plymouth to sort himself out . . . only to be run down in the Channel on his next departure. Despairing, he returned again for repair. And then the real blow struck: 'Lively Lady' fell away from the wall of the dock just when she was nearly ready to put to sea again. This time the damage was severe and the 'match' with Chichester had to be abandoned. Chichester left and Rose went back to his work – and to making 'Lively Lady' ready for the oceans once again.

The next year he was off. On 16th July 1967 Alec Rose and 'Lively Lady' sailed from Portsmouth. Very nearly a whole year later, he returned – a little disappointed in his time but blaming himself rather than his boat, despite the battering they had both received from headwinds and the frustrations of weeks of calms; nonetheless confessing to be well satisfied with what he described as the 'great adventure' of his life.

Later Rose, like Chichester before him, received a knighthood.

But young men sail round the world, too. Robin Knox-Johnston, a personable Merchant Navy officer in his late twenties, had built a solid $32\frac{1}{2}$ft (9.9m) ketch of Indian teak in which he intended to sail home from a posting in India. She was the yacht which should never have been built: Robin had sent off for plans but had received the wrong ones. There being no time to argue the toss, and these plans being of a seemingly robust little cruising yacht, the keel was laid. 'Suhaili', taking her name from a south-east wind in the Persian Gulf, came into being.

Knox-Johnston was on leave from the Merchant Navy in the spring of 1967 when the realization came that sooner or later someone would sail round the world non-stop. Chichester and Rose were both on the high seas and Knox-Johnston was determined that this last-remaining challenge should fall to a Briton. He felt the duty was his and discussed the building of a new, faster boat for the voyage but just could not raise the money. His mount had to be 'Suhaili' – and time was running short for by early 1968 the Sunday Times newspaper had announced the Golden Globe Trophy and the

Alec Rose arriving in Portsmouth at the end of his 354-day round the world voyage. *Central Press Photos Ltd*

£5,000 prize money which would go to the first singlehander to sail round the world non-stop.

Others had announced their intentions to join battle: John Ridgeway in 'English Rose IV', Commander Bill King in 'Galway Blazer' and Chay Blyth, who was Ridgeway's partner in a row across the Atlantic. Still more were to set sail: Loick Fougeron in the cutter 'Captain Browne', Nigel Tetley in the 40ft (12m) trimaran 'Victress', the ill-fated Donald Crowhurst in another 'Victress tri', Alex Carozzo in a 66ft (20m) ketch 'Gancia Americano' and Cape Horner Bernard Moitessier who had already circumnavigated in 'Joshua', named after his hero Slocum.

In June 1968, at about the time that Rose was returning from his sojourn on the high seas, Knox-Johnston set out from Falmouth, one and two weeks behind Blyth and Ridgeway respectively and a couple of months ahead of most of the faster metal. His ingenious self-steering gear which he had nicknamed 'The Admiral' (for reasons he declines to divulge, as a

Merchant Navy officer) proved to have the temperament of a prima donna and gave up the ghost completely when the journey was less than half completed. His subsequent lash-up on the boat's main rudder, which itself was showing distressing signs of strain, saw him through the rest of the marathon, but he describes the cat's cradle as resembling one of 'Heath Robinson's nightmares'.

Even before his steering problems became acute, Knox-Johnston was considering giving up the whole idea of a non-stop circumnavigation and putting into Cape Town to effect some seamanlike repairs. A persistent leak had shown signs of worsening and had been repaired by the skipper during a period of calm. Without breathing apparatus, he had spent hours diving to fill a seam in the planking and to cover it with a copper patch, pausing only to shoot an over-inquisitive shark which was hampering operations.

Only the news that one of his closest rivals, Ridgeway, had retired to Brazil kept him going – going

Robin Knox-Johnston who in 1968/69 won the Golden Globe Trophy for being the first person to sail non-stop single-handed round the world.

Naomi James on the deck of her yacht 'Express Crusader'. *London Express*

towards a knockdown off the Cape of Good Hope and towards failure of his radio transmitter shortly thereafter. Fortunately he could still receive news from the outside world – he still had weather forecasts and snippets of news on the progress of others in the race. He learned when Blyth retired, when others started. He did not learn, until after weeks of battling with an invisible competitor, that Bernard Moitessier, with whom the world had believed he was racing neck and neck, had gone into orbit and carried on after rounding the Horn, to sail into the Indian Ocean and subsequently to drop his hook off Tahiti.

At one stage Knox-Johnston went aground. Yes, went aground on a non-stop circumnavigation. Skirting close to New Zealand, to try to rendezvous with his link-man from the Sunday Mirror newspaper, 'Suhaili's' keel touched the sandy bottom on a falling tide. But there's some silver inside most clouds and this brief hiatus did at least give the skipper time to free a jammed halyard.

Ten and a half months later, he returned to his port of departure, winner of the Golden Globe, first man to sail singlehanded and non-stop round the world. In his book 'A World of My Own', he describes the first official words which were spoken to him:–

'The first people to board were Her Majesty's Customs and Excise officers from Falmouth. As they jumped across, the senior officer, trying to keep a straight face, asked the time-honoured question: "Where from?"

"Falmouth" I replied.'

But Knox-Johnston did not claim his £5,000 prize money. Instead he supported an appeal which had been opened in memory of fellow-competitor Donald Crowhurst. Crowhurst's trimaran 'Teignmouth Electron' had been found, all sails set, in the Atlantic but of Crowhurst there was no sign. Comparisons were inevitably drawn with the 'Marie Celeste' and as the evidence contained in the ship's log was pieced together it became apparent that the psychological pressure had proved too great for 'Electron's' skipper. He had apparently faked his reported positions and in fact had never left the Atlantic. His own fate was never known.

Knox-Johnston, on the other hand, was pronounced 'distressingly normal' after both pre- and post-race psychiatric examinations.

The ladies must not be forgotten. Each new marathon venture brings its share of lady skippers.

First girl to sail singlehanded across the Atlantic was Nicolette Milnes Walker in the 8-year-old, 30ft (9m) Pionier 'Aziz', but she did not compete in the OSTAR. She completed her voyage in 1971, rather than risk being beaten by waiting for the 1972 race, because she desperately wanted to be the first solo girl across and she

Clare Francis celebrates her arrival after the OSTAR: first girl, second British Boat. *Rob Humphreys*

'ADC Accutrac', Clare Francis's yacht for the Whitbread Round the World Race, 1977/78. *Ajax News Photos*

knew that she could not afford to campaign a larger, faster boat which might beat other girls in the race.

A research psychologist in her late twenties, Nicolette had a secondary reason for the trip: she was interested to find out what it was really like to be alone at sea. It was a good job she kept a detailed record, for she admits to remembering nothing of the voyage under the barrage of interview and press receptions which were showered upon her after her arrival in the USA!

Petite Clare Francis apparently had everything. In her mid-twenties she boasted a good job, an expense account, a car and a flat. But she felt the need to be alone, to go away and Do Something. So, a sailor from the age of five, she put all her money into the purchase of a Nicholson 32 and set off to cross the Atlantic. Like Nicolette Milnes Walker, she chose the southerly Azores route. Unlike Nicolette, she followed her marathon with others: the two-handed Round Britain Race, the Azores Race and the French L'Aurore singlehanded race, before finding sponsorship from a jam-making company for her OSTAR attempt in the Ohlson 38 'Robertson's Golly' in 1976 – she was the first girl to finish at 13th and sixth in class on corrected time. She even found the strength to take a film which recorded, not just the achievements and exciting

moments but also the utter misery she felt in the awful gales she experienced. The film is enough to send the weekend sailor straight round to see the membership secretary of his local golf club.

Clare has described a sickness – not a seasickness but a singlehanded sickness, a loneliness and tension which disrupts the human system. She has said of the sailor on land that he would rather be at sea: of the sailor at sea that he would rather be on land.

But none of it stopped her driving a fully-crewed yacht in the Round the World Race of 1977/78.

And what can be said of the staggering performance of Naomi James, daughter of a New Zealand sheep farmer, married to an Englishman. At twenty-nine years old she sailed solo right round the world in a 53-footer (16m) – beating the record of Sir Francis Chichester into the bargain.

She left the UK on 9th September 1977 and sailed into Dartmouth on 8th June 1978 to a tumultuous welcome, having completed her circumnavigation in just 272 days. Freshly groomed and looking most attractive, she confessed surprise at the size of the welcoming party – and straight away started talking of her plans to enter the 1980 Observer Singlehanded trans-Atlantic Race. A far cry from sheep farming!

Glossary

Abaft: on the after side of.

Aft: towards or near the stern.

Aft pulpit: *see* PULPIT.

Astern: (1) in the direction of the stern; (2) after of the vessel.

Athwart, Athwartships: at right angles to the centreline.

Ballast: weight, usually of metal but can be of concrete, placed low in a boat to provide stability.

Bear away: put the helm up so that the boat alters course away from the wind (opp. luff up).

Bermudan Sloop: boat rigged with a single triangular (Bermudan) mainsail and a single foresail.

Bilge: the part of the hull where sides and bottom meet.

Bilge-keeler: boat with shallow keels attached to the bilge to provide lateral resistance and a measure of stability, usually in place of a fin keel.

Block: common abbreviation for pulley block, which can be wood, metal or plastic.

Bolt rope: rope sewn to the edges of a sail to add strength and discourage fraying, as 'luff rope'.

Boom Vang: *see* KICKING STRAP.

Bow: forward part of a vessel.

Brace (Aus): *see* GUY.

Bridge deck: area of a deck which it is necessary to cross in order to go from one section of a vessel to another.

Buoyancy: upward thrust exerted by the water on a vessel that supports its weight. Reserve buoyancy is provided by extra hull volume available above the waterline to support any increase in displacement anywhere along the hull.

Carvel: edge-to-edge planking giving a smooth hull surface.

Caulk or Calk: fill the seams of a boat to prevent leaks.

Centreboard or centreplate: wooden board or metal plate lowered through a slot in the bottom to reduce leeway.

Chain pipe: pipe on the foredeck through which the chain passes.

Chine: the angle, joint or structural member within the joint where two flat hull panels meet.

Chopped strand mat: unwoven glass cloth used in boat building to strengthen polyester resin.

Cleat: T-shape device used for securing the tail of a rope. Patent device, sometimes with moving jaws (jamming cleat) for performing the same function.

Clew: lower outer corner of sail to which sheet is attached.

Clinker-built or Lapstrake: hull construction in which adjacent planks overlap each other.

Close-hauled: sailing as close to the wind as possible.

Corrected time: theoretical time arrived at after applying a handicap to the lapsed time in which a yacht completes a race.

Counter: that part of the stern which overhangs the water.

Cutter: single-masted sailing vessel with more than one headsail, gaff-rigged or bermudan-rigged.

Daggerboard: centreboard which does not pivot but is raised and lowered vertically.

Deadrise or Rise of Floor: the amount of rise of the bottom between the top of the keel and the chine or turn of the bilge.

Development class: a class with very few basic rules within which design development is encouraged.

Displacement: weight of water displaced by a floating vessel, which is the same as the weight of the vessel itself.

Double diagonal: two layers of planks, each laid diagonally to the keel but at right angles to each other.

Fair: line or surface which is smooth and without abrupt or awkward changes of direction, bumps and hollows.

Fair-in: remove any bumps and hollows in a curved surface.

Fairlead: fitting through which a line runs; it guides or alters the direction of the lead of the line.

Fiddle: a rail fitted to the edge of a horizontal surface to prevent objects sliding off when the vessel heels or rolls.

Fifty-fifty: another name for a motor-sailer, so called because it is half a sailing boat and half a motor cruiser.

Fin keel: a keel which does not form an integral part of the hull shape; usually attached after the hull is completed.

Fixed rudder: a rudder whose blade and stock is/are one-piece or immovable, so that the blade may not be moved relative to the hull other than by removing the rudder from the transom fittings.

Flies a hull: term used to describe a catamaran heeling so that one hull is out of the water.

Foot: lower edge of a sail.

Fore: in, or towards, or nearer the bows.

Foredeck: deck forward of the mast.

Foresail: also headsail, in general terms any sail tacked down forward of the mast; in racing dinghies synonymous with jib or genoa.

Forestay: any stay led forward of a mast.

Forward or Forrard: (1) forward part of a vessel, near the bows; (2) nearer the bows, as 'forward of'.

Frame: (1) transverse structural member to which the hull planking or shell is secured; (2) skeleton of a vessel.

Full keel: similar to a long keel but of a squarer shape in profile.

Fully-battened: a sail whose battens run full length from luff to leech.

Gaff: spar to which the upper edge of a sail is attached.

Galley: kitchen area.

Gel coat: first coat of resin applied to a mould when producing a glassfibre moulding. If a coloured moulding is required, pigment is added.

Gimbals: system by which an object is suspended and pivoted in one direction, or two directions at right angles to each other in the horizontal plane, so that the object remains horizontal regardless of the attitude of the vessel; usually used for the compass and cooking stove.

Gooseneck: universal joint which connects the boom to the mast.

Grapple: type of small anchor with a stork and four arms in a star form which works by hooking onto some obstacle rather than by its weight.

Ground tackle: anchors, cables, etc.

Guardrails or lifelines: safety rails fitted around a boat through stanchions to prevent the crew falling overboard.

Gudgeon: a fitting with a hole in it which takes the pin of a pintle on which the rudder pivots.

Gunter rig: a gaff slides up a short mast and forms an extension of the mast. The sail has four sides but appears to be triangular.

Gunwales or gunnels (US: also rail): upper edge of the sides of a vessel.

Guy: steadying rope for a spar, etc. Spinnaker guy (UK & US) controls the fore-and-aft position of the spinnaker pole (Aus: Brace); foreguy holds the spinnaker pole forward and down.

Gybe (jibe): change tacks with the wind aft.

Halyards or Halliards: ropes used to hoist sails, flags, etc.

Handicap fleet: Fleet of boats in a handicap race.

Hard chine: as opposed to round bilge, the topsides meet the bottom at an angle instead of a curve.

Headboard: a piece of stiffening, usually of wood, metal, or plastics, sewn into the head of a sail.

Heading: direction in which a vessel is going.

Heel: (1) to list or lean over; (2) base of mast or centreboard.

Hiking (US & AUS): *see* SITTING OUT.

Hiking board (US): *see* SLIDING SEAT.

Hiking stick (US): *see* TILLER EXTENSION.

Hiking straps (US): *see* TOESTRAPS.

Hounds: the point on the mast below the masthead where forestay is attached.

Hull: the structure, the body of a vessel.

Jib: the forwardmost fore-and-aft headsail.

Kedge (US: Lunch Hook): (1) light additional anchor usually used for short stops; (2) to kedge off is to lay out the kedge away from a vessel so that she can be moved by hauling on the line attached to it, esp. after running aground.

Keel: centreline backbone of a vessel to which the frames, timbers and floors are attached.

Ketch: two-masted sailing boat with the smaller mizzen mast stepped forward of the rudder post.

Kicking Strap (US Vang): a wire strop, tackle or similar device used to hold the main boom at the desired level and prevent it skying due to the force of wind in the mainsail.

Launching tube (US): *see* SPINNAKER CHUTE.

Lay up: build up layers of glass fibres and resin in the construction of a mould or boat.

Leeboards: boards lowered on either side of a flat-bottomed vessel to reduce leeway.

Leech (US: also Leach): (1) after edge of a triangular sail; (2) the two side edges of a square sail.

Lee Helm: a boat 'carrying' this has a tendency to bear away, which can be righted by holding the helm to leeward.

Leeward: downwind; the direction to which the wind is blowing; away from the wind. Opposite of windward.

Lifting rudder: any rudder whose blade may be raised partially or wholly without removing the stock from the transom.

Long keel: runs the full length of the boat underneath from bow to stern.

Loose-footed: said of a sail only attached to either end of the boom by tack and clew, and not along the length of the boom.

Luff: (n.) the leading edge of a sail.

Luff: (v.) to turn the vessel towards the wind.

Lug: (1) fore-and-aft sail with a yard, part of which extends forward of the mast; (2) US: carry too much sail.

Lunch hook: *See* KEDGE.

Mainsail: sail set on the mast, or the main mast if there is more than one mast.

Mainsheet: sheet which controls the mainsail.

Mast gate: a minor structural member, usually hinged, which helps to hold a mast in position at deck level.

Mast step: the piece of wood or metal fabrication which locates the heel of the mast, or the recess in which the heel rests.

Mizzen or Mizen: fore-and-aft sail set on the mizzen mast.

Motor-sailer: boat designed to perform reasonably well under sail or power.

Mould: a structure used to give a hull its final shape.

Moulded or Molded Hull: a hull constructed by laying a number of skins of thin wood in succession.

Mud bearth: a shore mooring, usually a hollow in soft mud, where a boat may be kept when it is laid up.

Navigatorium: navigation area.

One-design: a term used to describe a class in which all the boats are of a single design, at least in respect of hull and rig.

Open meeting: race meeting run by a yacht club in which entry is not restricted to club members.

Outrigger: subsidiary hull set outboard of the main hull to provide stability.

Overhangs: the parts of the bow and stern which extend beyond the waterline.

Overlap: a technical racing term used when two yachts are racing on a parallel course and some part of one yacht's hull or equipment is forward of some part of the other yacht's hull or equipment.

Pintle: a fitting with a pin which locates in a hole in a gudgeon and on which the rudder pivots. Attached to the stern or rudder post and to the rudder.

Pipecot: a framework or pipe with canvas stretched within, forming a sleeping berth which can be folded up against the hull.

Plane: a fast, lightweight racing dinghy can achieve speeds at which the hull will lift and skim across the surface of the water supported on her own bow wave. She is said to be planing. While planing, a dinghy can achieve higher speeds than are possible while displacement sailing (when the hull is immersed to its normal waterline).

Plug: master shape used to make moulds which are used in the construction of glass fibre yachts.

Pole: (1) true north and south; (2) the spinnaker pole is a spar used to extend the spinnaker to windward.

Pram bow: flattened rather than pointed bow with a transom across it.

Pulpit: metal guardrail fitted at bows or stern to provide security for the crew working in the ends of a boat.

Rail (US): *see* GUNWALE.

Rating: a vessel is measured and given a rating which enables her to take part in handicap races.

Reef: (n.) the amount of sail which is disposed of by the act of reefing.

Reef: (v.) to reduce sail area by gathering in a portion of the sail, rolling it tightly and tying it out of the way.

Release agent: a non-stick coating painted on the inside of a mould to stop the next coating, a gel, from sticking.

Restricted class: class in which certain measurements are specified, but other aspects are left free for individual design and development.

Ribs: timbers of a vessels to which the planking is fastened.

Rigging: all the wires and ropes used to support masts and to control sails and yards, sub-divided into standing and running rigging.

Rise of Floor: *see* DEADRISE.

Roach: curved area of leech in a fore-and-aft sail which extends beyond the direct line from head or peak to clew.

Rubbing strake or rubber (US & AUS: Rub Rail): strip fitted outside the topstrake to protect the sides from damage.

Rub Rail (US & AUS): *see* RUBBING STRAKE.

Rudder: flat vertical surface at the stern which is turned by the tiller or wheel to alter the course of a vessel.

Scantlings: dimensions of timbers used in the construction of a boat.

Section: shape of a boat when cut in any direction, longitudinally, horizontally or vertically, but usually taken as athwartships.

Self-Bailing (US): *see* SELF-DRAINING.

Self-draining cockpit (US: also Self-bailing): cockpit with holes that allow the water to run out automatically.

Self-steering gear: apparatus by which a vessel steers herself unattended.

Shackle: metal link with a removable bolt, of various shapes such as D, U, bow, twisted.

Sheave: the wheel-like part of a block over which the rope runs.

Sheet: rope (or wire) used to control a sail.

Shroud plate: the fitting attached to the hull to which the shroud is connected. Synonymous with chainplate.

Shrouds: standing rigging which supports the mast athwartships.

Sidedeck: deck around the sides of the vessel; specifically aft of the main mast.

Sitting out: (US & AUS: Hiking): to sit on the windward side of the boat with body weight as far outboard as necessary to keep the boat upright.

Sliding Seat (US: Hiking Board): Board which slides across the crew's quarters to enable him to place his weight as far outboard as possible to keep the boat level.

Sloop: (modern definition) fore-and-aft sailing craft with one mast and only one headsail. Archaically: any small, sleek sailing vessel.

Slot and Tab: boat building construction in which tabs of pre-shaped panels slot into other panels and the joins are glass-taped.

Slot effect: obtained when the mainsail and jib are sheeted in such a way that the airflow over the leeward side of the mainsail is faster than otherwise and turbulance is reduced.

Spill the wind: allow some wind to escape from a sail to ease the pressure.

Spinnaker: a large, lightweight sail set when the wind is free.

Spinnaker chute (UK); Launching tube (US): tube out of which a spinnaker is hoisted, fitted to small racing craft.

Spinnaker pole: a pole or boom whose outboard end supports the spinnaker clew, either directly or via the guy, when the inboard end is clipped to the mast.

Stanchion: metal post bolted to the deck to support lifelines or guardrails.

Staysail: triangular sail the luff of which is attached to a stay.

Stem dinghy: a rowing dinghy with a pointed bow.

Stitch and glue: boat building construction in which pre-shaped hull panels are sewn together with copper wire and held together with glass-fibre tape over the join.

Strip planking: small planks laid edge to edge around a framework and glued and nailed to each other as well as the boat's frame.

Swinging Strap (Aus): *see* TOESTRAP.

Tack (n.)(1) the forward lower corner of a sail, by which it is attached to the vessel or spur; (2) the act of turning; (3) one leg of a zig-zagging course to windward (sometimes called a BOARD).

Tack (v.): (1) to attach a sail to the vessel or to a spar; (2) to turn the vessel with her bow towards the direction of the wind; (3) to shape a course to windward by zig-zagging, sailing close hauled with the wind first on one side, then the other.

Tactics: a series of skilful manoeuvres used in competition.

Taking up: said of a planked wooden boat when the wood swells in the water and the seams close.

Tender: (1) small dinghy used to ferry the crew of a larger vessel;

(2) (opp. stiff), a vessel which heels easily.

Thwarts: athwartship seats in a dinghy.

Tiller: bar connected to the rudder to steer the vessel.

Tiller Extension (US: Hiking stick): extension to the tiller for use when sitting or hiking out.

Toestrap: (US: Hiking Strap; Aus: Swinging Strap) straps under which the crew hook their feet so that they can sit, or hike, outboard.

Transom: flat or curved surface extending across the aft end of a vessel. Some craft, especially small dinghies, also have a transom forward.

Triple skin: construction formed of three layers of boat-building material, usually planks.

Turtle: bag from which a spinnaker may be hoisted.

Twin keel: two keels, one on either side of the central line, but no central keel.

Twist: the alteration of the angle of tack of one part of the mainsail over the rest.

Una rig: only one sail.

Unstayed: without the wires or ropes which support a mast in the fore-and-aft direction.

Vang (US): *see* KICKING STRAP.

Weather helm: a boat 'carrying' this has a tendency to turn into the wind, which can be righted by holding the tiller towards the windward side of the boat.

Windward: towards the wind, opposite of leeward.

Woven roving: woven glass fibre cloth used in boat building to strengthen polyester resin.

Yawl: two-masted for-and-aft rigged vessel, the mizzen mast being stepped aft of the rudder post (cf. ketch).

Index